Homeschooling High School
with College in Mind

Dedication

I dedicate this book to my husband, who has been an active supporter of all of our homeschooling adventures through the years. He has also been my chief cheerleader as I started to blog, and later, to write this book.

I would also like to thank Vicki Tillman, MA, from 7 Sisters Homeschool, who encouraged me to write about homeschooling high school. She taught me so much and has been such an encouragement along the way.

I also must mention Tricia Hodges, from Hodgepodge, who patiently taught me how to blog while serving as my editor for The Curriculum Choice.

Most importantly, I would like to thank you, my readers, for your encouragement to write, as without readers, I could not be a writer. AND it is a joy to be even a small part of your homeschooling adventures.

And I also dedicate this book to children. May their spirits continue to grow and thrive and may they become all that they were meant to be.

For more tips on homeschooling high school and college:

- I invite you subscribe to my blog, **BJ's Homeschool** at *www.bjshomeschool.com*
- And to join my Facebook group --**College Discussions for Homeschoolers**, where you can meet other moms of college bound homeschoolers.
- I can be reached on **Facebook – BJ's Homeschool** here: www.facebook.com/betsyhomeschoolcoach/
- You are welcome to follow me on **Pinterest – BJ's Homeschool** at *www.pinterest.com/betsysproger* for updates on college and encouragement and resources.

Table of Contents

Introduction

When Betsy asked me to write an introduction for her new book, I was delighted to support her. I first met Betsy on Facebook, when I asked a homeschooling high school group where their favorite college advice could be found. "BJ's Homeschool!" was the rousing response.

Following this advice, I eagerly read her blog and found that Betsy has a wealth of understanding and knowledge to share with the parents of college bound homeschoolers. Obviously, her been-there, done-that experience with her daughter is invaluable.

But since her teen went off on her own, Betsy has shared her expertise with thousands of homeschooling families through her blog, the Facebook group - College Discussions for Homeschoolers, and through one-to-one mentoring with homeschool parents needing more personalized help.

Many home educators give up homeschooling after 8th grade, because they mistakenly think that the more advanced subjects are too hard to teach or that colleges will not accept a parent-made transcript. This could not be further from the truth.

Advanced classes can be found on the internet, in summer intensive programs, through part-time high school, or dual-enrollment college classes. Unlike even five years ago when my sons graduated, more and more four-year colleges have admissions officers who are not only open to homeschooled students, but actively seek them out. Many have dedicated homeschool admissions officers, who are adept at reading parent-written transcripts and value the insight into our students that parent educators can provide.

In this book, Betsy provides support, encouragement and step-by-step advice on all aspects of the homeschool high school and college application process. I've used her section-by-section guidance on creating transcripts and completing the Common Application, for students and parent/counselors, with many of my own homeschool families.

I'm so glad that she has collected all her advice into such an easy to use format. This book is a must-read for parents considering homeschooling high school and for parents in the thick of the application process.

by Lessa Scherrer, College Advisor at College Inside Track
Certificate in College Counseling, UCLA

--Mrs. Scherrer specializes in helping students find their best fit college and has lots of experience working with homeschooled applicants, as well as students with learning differences.

Chapter 1

Skipping Public School all the way to College

My husband and I began our homeschooling journey when our daughter was 4 years old. She was so ready for kindergarten but too young to go. At the same time, she was already doing math problems and showing signs of wanting to learn academically.

So we took the plunge early.

Preparing to Homeschool

I read about homeschooling, talked with my friends who were doing it, got ideas for curriculum from them, and joined a local homeschool support group to meet others who were homeschooling. All of these things helped build up my confidence for taking on homeschooling.

One of the most helpful books that I found as a newbie homeschooler was the *Unofficial Guide to Homeschooling* by Kathy Ishizuka. It included discussions on making the decision to homeschool, how to go about learning about your state's homeschool regulations, and much more.

State Homeschool Laws

As Washington State homeschoolers, we found out that there were no regulations until our child turned 8. After that, our state law listed the subjects that needed to be covered each year, including an annual testing requirement.

Each state has their own laws on homeschooling, and they are quite varied. Some states ask for annual testing while others do not. Washington State allowed us to test our own child at home.

There are a few states that ask for portfolios to be made of the child's work, which is then sent into the school district for review. To find out your state's homeschooling law requirements, a good source Home School Legal Defense Association (HSLDA).

When I first looked at that site, I was overwhelmed. But I found out that it was not hard to deal with our law. And homeschooling gave us the freedom to choose what curriculum we wanted to use, and how we wanted to approach it.

That freedom was priceless as we went about figuring out how to meet our daughter's needs, especially when it came to learning resources and curriculum.

One of the first things I did to find curriculum for my child, was to visit our local teacher's bookshop. There they had a number of resources for all ages, up to 8th grade. I just picked out a few preschool/early learning books, with my daughter's help. For instance, if she was interested in a certain animal, we got materials on that animal. Of course, the library was a great resource, too.

That was how we got started. Then later we began to familiarize ourselves with some of the homeschool curricula that was out there.

Homeschool Curriculum Resources

If you are looking for homeschool curricula ideas, there is a site called *Cathy Duffy Reviews*, that has been going strong for years, and has reviews on almost everything homeschool related right there.

The *Rainbow Resource* site also has a plethora of creative homeschool resources. I have often turned to them for less traditional ideas. I loved their literature guides, so many to choose from.

I also write homeschool curriculum reviews on a site called *The Curriculum Choice*, which features reviews by homeschool moms who have used the resources in their homeschool. These reviews are mostly Christian focused, my reviews are mostly secular.

Some of the faith-based curriculum that we liked, and were good for our daughter, could also be modified so that they could be used in a secular way as well.

More Curriculum and Homeschooling Resources

Over the years, I have gathered together my favorite resources for different ages on my blog. If you go to BJ's Homeschool, just click on the tabs for The Early Years, (Preschool to 6th grade), Middles and High School to give you some ideas of what we did when. It includes lots of information and reviews of our favorite homeschool curriculum.

What about that often-cited question of socialization?

Homeschool Support Groups/Community Activities

Once we had our curricula, we started to look around for a homeschool support group to join. I wanted to connect with other moms who had been there and done that, and of course I wanted my daughter to meet other kids her own age.

We found a local support group in our area and went to their monthly meetings. *The Homeschool Mom* site also has support groups listed by state and city if you want to connect with one in your area.

Since our group only met monthly, I searched around for another social activity or two for my daughter. We found some at our local Parks Department, and then decided to join a music movement group.

My daughter loved those classes, as they involved a lot of movement, and she was a VERY active kid. It became such a good way for her to make her first "school" friends.

So by reading up on homeschooling, learning about our state homeschool laws, exploring curricula, and then finding a support group to join, we built up our confidence for homeschooling. And I am so glad that we did.

Had we gone the public school route, we would have had the usual challenges of getting our 2e daughter's unique learning issues met and addressed there, but at home we could accommodate for her attentional issues, sensory needs, and her difficulty with auditory processing.

After graduating from our homeschool, our daughter went directly to a 4-year college. She was accepted into each of the colleges on her list, with scholarship offers. That included a state college, a private faith-based college, a tier one University, and one more. This was all done through her homeschool transcript.

It was a thrill to watch her present her research capstone during her university's Honors Colloquium.

Just sharing that joy to encourage you. Homeschooling prepared our teen very well for college, and yes, I was that mom. Worried that we miss something, that our brand of education was not up to college standards, etc. But I was so wrong.

When our teen got to college, she made the Dean's List her first quarter and many quarters after that.

We are so glad that we decided to homeschool through high school, and below, in the next chapter, are some of the reasons that we did.

Chapter 2

101 Reasons to Homeschool High School

Our daughter was thriving and busy discovering her strengths and special interests during her middle school years. Deciding to continue with homeschooling during the high school was not a hard decision for us.

Yes, it took some extra organizing and record keeping, and a few sleepless nights, where we worried if we had made the right decision for our daughter.

But we went with our hearts, and we found that homeschooling high school gave our daughter SO many benefits.

On the top of the list, it allowed her lots of time to get to know who she was and explore her interests and participate in activities. These activities helped her to find out what she wanted to do in life, and also led her to find her major in college.

That's our #1 reason why we homeschooled high school.

Here's 100 more. I kept this list close by, when we had *those* difficult days....

1. To be there during the important teen years, while your child is exploring possibilities and discovering who they are.

2. To be able to take time off for vacation anytime in the year.

3. To be able to re-evaluate and adjust things as you go along.

4. To build up our teens.

5. To be able to make their own transcript, using your own grading scale.

6. To have a better chance in getting into college, as courses can be redone, or taken at a slower pace, for better learning and a chance to get a higher GPA.

7. To teach your teen the love of learning.

8. And that making mistakes is a part of it all.

9. To guide our teens, act as mentors and offer resources to help develop their interests and gifts.

10. To create time for special interests, like programming, photography, filmmaking, etc.

11. To allow your teen to work at his/her own pace.

12. To be the one to choose your teen's curriculum/activities with them.

13. For 1 on 1 learning.

14. To be able to make your own homemade courses.

15. To build in "goof-off" fun times for your teen to still be a "kid".

16. To get to watch your teen as they learn and develop as an individual.

17. To set up the daily schedule as you want for your teen.

18. To take time for handwork, birdwatching, or something else.

19. To be there, when deep conversations naturally occur.

20. To have lots of time for electives.

21. To be able to explore unique activities.

22. To build leadership skills.

23. To do service and volunteering in the community.

24. To take time for meals and eat when our teens need to.

25. To be able to guide them as they explore the possibilities in the world around them.

26. To decide when to take a break.

27. To be able to teach family values and morals.

28. To avoid busy work.

29. To have the ability to choose where to study, at a park, at the library, etc.

30. To avoid having to sit at a classroom desk all day, and to study in the way that fits your teen's needs.

31. To have your teen attend a homeschool prom.

32. To allow teens to be themselves, to develop as individuals, instead of being a member of a clique.

33. To learn in a supportive, non-pressurized environment.

34. To have a soft place to fall, for your teen.

35. Avoid having to teach to the test.

36. To be able to dive deeply into a subject of interest.

37. To be able to learn together.

38. Encourage their own thinking.

39. To be able to make your own courses.

40. Have more time for electives!

41. To have hands-on learning opportunities.

42. To develop sibling relationships and keep them strong.

43. Continue with your own homeschooling style.

44. To learn history as it happened, not dependent upon a curriculum chosen by "experts".

45. For teen-led learning!

46. To do nature study whenever you want.

47. All of your teen's learning counts towards high school credit.

48. To be able to study math, without having to use the newest standard math approach.

49. To allow teens to mature at their own pace.

50. Closer family relationships.

51. To be less affected by peer pressuring.

52. To take breaks when needed.

53. Can use online, textbooks, living literature, whatever works best.

54. To set up your day however you want such as even doing night school.

55. To grow life-long hobbies and interests.

56. To keep their sense of wonder and creativity.

57. Can study at the park.

58. To inspire and promote their interests.

59. To provide a college prep education, high school, vocational or special needs education, in the way that fits your teen best, within a nurturing environment.

60. To do art and music studies.

61. To go on field trips!

62. To have meaningful contact with other adults in the community.

63. To be able to adapt the teaching style for ADD, ADHD, dyslexia, autism, Aspersers, etc.

64. To have time for free reading.

65. To be able to take care of medical issues at home.

66. To have time to reconnect and get out in nature together.

67. To do apprenticeships.

68. To take lunch break whenever your teens are hungry.

69. For co-ops and homeschool group activities.

70. To be there, to nurture your teens emotional and spiritual development.

71. To help them begin to find their direction and purpose in life.

72. To be able to create their own study space.

73. To avoid the early morning rush to the bus.

74. To teach good nutrition, by cooking together.

75. To foster healthy and supportive relationships.

76. To build strong connections that will last through college and beyond.

77. To be able to design your teen's high school education, without having to follow public school requirements.

78. To be able to plan your teen's high school years yourself.

79. To know your teen's friends...

80. To help your teen develop appreciation for the simple things in life.

81. To have the time for your teen to listen to their heart.

82. To teach life skills.

83. Able to monitor your teen's activities much better.

84. To focus on your teen's strengths.

85. To have fun with your teen.

86. To help guide your teen's friendships.

87. To be able to guide your teen's steps to college, vocational training, or work.

88. For character development.

89. Flexibility.

90. To have your teen's dad be a part of her education.

91. Can repeat a class.

92. Going on vacation during the off-season.

93. No busywork.

94. Less pressure to conform to latest fashions.

95. Hot chocolate is available anytime.

96. Can study on the couch, with the cat, or laying down on the floor.

97. Build confidence.

98. To be your teen's mentor, as they deal with the important teen years.

99. Because you know your teen best.

100. Because you can build your relationship with your teen...

And finally,

101. To build special memories that you will treasure always.... As you know, homeschooling makes tons of them!

Chapter 3

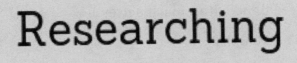

When we were in the middle school years, my husband and I began thinking about the possibility of college for our daughter.

And I was more than a little nervous. But I wanted my teen to have the option of going directly to a 4-year college, if she felt that was the way that she wanted to go.

How would I, as a homeschooling mom, help her get there?

The idea of knocking on the college door with a homeschool transcript in hand was *more* than a little daunting for me. I knew that the homeschool transcript was now widely accepted by colleges, but the colleges seemed so big and I, in contrast felt so small.

Do you ever feel that way?

I wanted more information, so I began to research about homeschoolers and college. I found that there were many homeschool friendly colleges out there that wanted the type of kids that homeschooling produces – motivated and independent learners. Seeing that spurred me to want to find out more.

What would my daughter need to do to be considered for college acceptance?

I looked up the most likely colleges that my daughter might attend. The college entrance requirements were similar, but not consistent from college to college. Some colleges had extra requirements for their homeschooling applicants, and some didn't.

What's a parent to do?

This chapter explains how we came up with the list of required courses that my teen would need for college admission. And it wasn't that hard to do!

Our first step in going from homeschool to college was to research our daughter's college entrance requirements.

Starting research on this early is a help, but it is still possible to do this any time in high school by simply recalling information from their previous requirements, and going from there. And you can always add in an extra quarter or two, to make up for any requirements that you might have missed.

College Entrance Requirements

Each college will show their admission requirements with just a click of a button. This information was easy for us to find. All you have to do is look at the prospective college's website and click on the *freshman admission requirements.* We found these requirements to be similar from college to college, with only some variance depending if the college was an Ivy league, private, or a state college.

Freshman admission requirements can sometimes also be labeled College Academic Distribution Requirements (CADR).

College Academic Distribution Requirements (CADR)

All applicants must complete a minimum level of preparation in six subject areas. This requirement ensures that students entering the University have an appreciation for the liberal arts and are adequately prepared to succeed in college.

SAMPLE ADMISSION REQUIREMENTS

1 A STATE UNIVERSITY

Math - 3 credits
English - 4 credits
Social Studies - 3 credits
Science, with labs - 2 credits
Foreign Language - 2 credits
Senior Year Math or Statistics course - 1 credit
1/2 -1 credit of Fine Art

Here are more examples, just for comparison sake.

My niece is going to a faith-based college in our area. This is how her college entrance requirements looked:

#2 A PRIVATE CHRISTIAN COLLEGE

English - 4 credits
Math - 2 credits
Social Studies - 2 credits
Science - 2 credits
Foreign Language - 2 credits
Electives - 3 credits

You see that this college does not require as many credits as the first one did. That would leave more time for volunteering, or special interests, etc.

#3 AN IVY UNIVERSITY

English - 4 credits
Math - 4 credits
Science 4 credits, with 3 lab sciences
Social Studies – 4 credits
Foreign Language – 3 credits

See how they require so much more than the above two examples. Many ivies also look for SAT subject tests, and AP courses etc.

As you can easily see, each college is different.

Some colleges also require extra things from homeschool applicants. Our next step was to look for any of these specific requirements for homeschoolers. They didn't get in our way.

SPECIAL HOMESCHOOL REQUIREMENTS

To find out if your teen's prospective colleges have extra requirements for homeschoolers, just check on their websites. If there are none listed, I would also contact the Admissions office, just to be sure. Some colleges don't list them on their websites, but most do.

Validation

This term just means that the colleges are requiring something specifically for homeschool applicants, like a few outside credits or testing to "validate" the homeschool transcript.

Three of our colleges required what they called "validation" for certain subjects, but two of them have now dropped these extra requirements! Some colleges still have them, but the trend is towards dropping or simplifying them....

Below are 3 examples of homeschool requirements, and as you will see, they vary A LOT.

College A –
A Private Elite College

This one is still asking for lots of "validation".

"Homeschooled applicants need to show additional non-homeschool setting assessments, or validation in 3 areas, Math, Science, and Foreign Language......."

To do that, choose one of the following for each subject:

> 1. *Take an AP test or SAT subject test*
> 2. *OR take the ACT test*
> 3. *OR CLEP testing*
> 4. *OR take the course at an accredited college or community college, AND*
> 5. *For foreign language, take a test at the college*

What we did:

We just took the ACT test. That gave the college their "validation" for math and English. For foreign language, my daughter took the equivalency test at the college during her senior year of homeschool, and she was accepted.

Anyone can take AP tests. That means your student does not have to take the AP course. They can study at home using AP resources and then go in for testing.

This school was the hardest to deal with for us, but by using their ACT testing option we did not stress about their extra requirements.

College B -
A Tier Two State College

This college did not require any special homeschooling requirements or validation!

Currently, their website suggests that applicants show rigor in their work, such as with college level courses, AP courses, or community college courses in their high school years. They also looked for volunteer or work experience.

What we did: We did one dual credit course, and my daughter did volunteer work which she included on her college applications where she was accepted.

College C -
A State College

This college just asks that GED scores be submitted. They use these scores to "validate" the homeschool transcript. No other hoops to go through!

So you see how this works, and varies so much from college to college.

Did you know that we don't need to follow the public school high school graduation requirements?

As homeschoolers, we only need to follow the homeschool laws written by our state, and most of them leave the decision of what to do during high school to the parents.

Therefore, once you have the college requirements figured out, you can enjoy filling in extra time with your teen's special interests, volunteering, and high school activities.

Forms

College Entrance Requirements Form - This is for recording your teens requirements for college admissions. Base requirements from a sample of colleges that you are considering.

Now let's look at making an overall plan for high school, which can start at any time.

Chapter 4

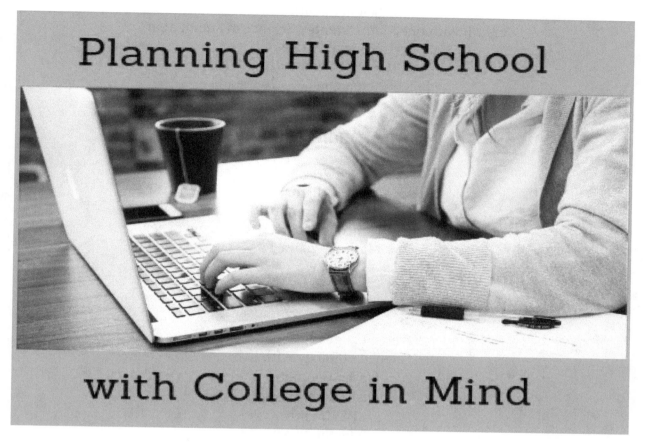

Planning High School with College in Mind

As homeschoolers, we are already experts in planning. We have searched for and chosen curriculum each year for our kids. And we have decided on which subjects to focus on and how to teach them to our kids.

Planning for high school with college in mind is really no different, except for one important thing... Now your teen has their college entrance requirements to fulfill.

This was overwhelming to us at first. But by laying out a tentative overall plan, I could relax and take it one step at a time.

Making an Overall High School Plan

With our list of admission requirements in hand, we sketched out what our high school years might look like... with our best guesses of what we wanted to do when. Our overall plan was flexible, and revised and reworked every year, as life happened.

Yet it was a helpful guide for us.

My Teen's College Entrance Requirements

4 English
2 Sciences with Lab
3 Math with one Math-oriented Science in Senior Year
3 Social Studies
2 Foreign Language
+ Electives to equal 24 - 26 credits

BJ's 4 YEAR HIGH SCHOOL PLAN

9th grade
World History
English (lit and composition)
Science - Physical Science (good prep for bio next year)
Math - Algebra 1
Elective
PE

10th grade
Foreign Language - Spanish 1
Science - Biology with Lab
Math - Geometry
English (lit and comp)
PE/Health
Take the PSAT

11th grade
Foreign Language - Spanish 2
US History
Science - Chemistry with lab
Math- Algebra 2
English
Elective
Take the SAT or ACT

12th grade
US Government
Science - Physics
English (lit and comp)
2 Electives
PE
Take SAT or ACT again if needed.

Your plan could be similar or entirely different from mine, depending on:

1. Your teen's entrance requirements
2. Special requirements for prospective math/science majors
3. Your homeschooling style

Making this plan helped us in 3 ways:

1. First, it helps keep organized all the requirements that need to be fulfilled, so that it does not become necessary to scramble in extra courses during senior year.

2. Secondly, it allows for the building of extracurricular interests, because core studies are already set in mind and on paper.

3. Thirdly, it gives confidence to push forward, and enjoy the high school years.

What if you don't know the exact college entrance requirements for your teen? In that case, you just have to make your best guesses when it comes to planning. Fulfilling these requirements still left a lot of time for special interests, activities and our electives, too.

Once we had our plan, we packed it away, and only brought it out when it was time for curriculum planning for next year. And it was revised each year, so we worked to follow our daughter's interests and needs.

It is nice to make your overall plan early on, if possible. However, if you are starting later you can still work on the overall plan, by just looking back and recording what has already been done and adding in the remaining courses needed.

Forms

Overall High School Plan Form – This form is for recording your best guesses of what courses you want to do when. It will help to satisfy the college entrance requirement.

Chapter 5

Choosing curriculum with college in mind... well, that really can't be hard for us. As homeschoolers, we are experts at choosing curriculum... it's almost a no brainer!!

As homeschoolers, we have searched for and picked out curricula each year for our kiddos. And we know how to tweak it to help it fit for our children's learning style, too.

There is just one important factor that is different for us, if we are aiming towards college...

Choosing curriculum for high school is really just the same, with one important difference....
Now there are the college admission requirements to think about as well.

With that information at hand, my daughter and I choose our curriculum one year at a time. And we found the whole process of choosing curricula to be very similar to our previous years!

Our Planning Process

We explored around, as usual, choosing the textbooks, living books, and/or online courses that would be a good fit for our teen. We worked to meet our teen's entrance requirements, but did not forget to focus on her special interests as well.

Following Your Teen's Interests

My daughter's interests in high school focused on film making, and political science. Therefore, we made sure to center her electives around those interests. ***But we found out that if she wanted to study either of these in college, the college entrance requirements would still be the same.***

She needed to complete her college entrance requirements in the basic subjects (English, social studies, math, foreign language and science), for either path.

Nevertheless, we still framed her electives around her interests. We even did a course in *Government* for one of her social studies requirements, and did outside activities centering around her interest in government as well. Later, photography and video making became more than one of her homemade electives.

We are eclectic homeschoolers who love unit studies, lots of hands-on learning, and mixing art into our academics.

Resources for your Curriculum Search:

1. CURRICULUM DIRECTORY at Let's Homeschool High School

The LetsHomeschoolHighSchool.com online curriculum directory is the most complete one I have seen! And it includes TONS of links!

2. THE CURRICULUM CHOICE

TheCurriculumChoice.com is full of curriculum reviews written by a team of authors (I am one) who have actually used the curriculum. It includes reviews of such curriculum as Tapestry of Grace, IEW, a number of Charlotte Mason options, and 1,000's more.

OUR FAVORITES FOR HIGH SCHOOL
CURRICULUM

SCIENCE

The typical requirements for college entrance include two science courses, usually Biology and Chemistry. If your student is headed towards a math, science, or programming major in college, they will likely be required to complete 4 lab sciences to be accepted.

Our college choices required two lab sciences. *We made sure that our choices included a science lab component.*

We decided to look for a structured course that included regular test-taking. Getting used to test-taking would help my daughter to prepare for later test-taking in college! We chose **Switched-On-Schoolhouse** (*SOS*), as we wanted a computer based program, and my daughter wanted to work independently. BONUS: all the lessons were graded for me.

SOS also offered tutoring (from their high school science teachers), to be purchased by the half hour. Working some of the science problems out with a teacher really helped when complex concepts came up. We also used **Home Science Tools** for our lab kits.

Other Science Options we considered:

Oak Meadow, A Beka, Lifepacs, Apologia Science which we found to be very strong.

MATH

Most of our college choices required Algebra 1, Geometry, and Algebra 2. (Or the series that Saxon offers, which is equivalent). My teen only needed to do 3 years of math.

If your teen is aiming towards math, computer programming, or a science major in college, they will likely be required to have 4 years of math, including Pre-Calculus in order for acceptance.

We looked at LifePacs, Switch-On-Schoolhouse, Math-You-See, A Beka, etc. We also considered Teaching Textbooks.

*It's all about what fits for **your** student.*

We found that Switched On Schoolhouse (SOS) fit our daughter's needs well. It had the structured and depth to help my daughter retain what she had learned. It also did a good job of providing the solid math background needed for the ACT, taken later on in junior year.

I like how this course is structured, with regular quizzes, giving my daughter practice in test taking.

All of the Alpha Omega Publications programs offer tutoring (including Monarch, Lifepacs, and SOS). There are now a number of online homework help/tutoring options, too.

Other Math options that we considered:

Check out The Curriculum Choice for a review of **ALEKS,** and also one on **No-Nonsense Algebra**. We also looked at **Mr. D's Math, Life of Fred, A Beka, Saxon** and **Khan Academy.**

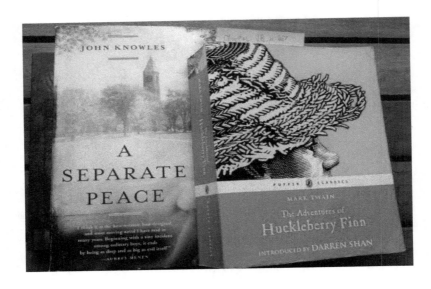

ENGLISH

Many of our colleges wanted something strong in literature and/or composition each year. One option to meet this requirement is to create your own literature course, and pick out the literature yourself. Pairing that with writing assignments can make a complete English course for your teen! For more information on how we did that, see the *Resources for Buyers* page.

We decided to go another way, and chose a ready-made course with good quality living literature. We chose **Oak Meadow** and **7 Sisters Homeschool** which both offer a variety of literature based courses, from 9th to 12th grade.

Both of these curriculum publishers, Oak Meadow and 7 Sisters include literary analysis and essay writing in their courses. We found that literary analysis helped my daughter to develop the critical thinking skills needed for college.

It also inspired wonderful, meaningful talks about literature. Many of my favorite high school memories were made during the afternoons, while sipping tea with my daughter and talking about the books that she had read. And that helped her to formulate ideas for her essays, too.

We liked using **7 Sisters Homeschool** for writing instruction. They offer many levels of essay writing courses, plus Speech Courses as well. Another popular choice for English is the **Institute of Excellence in Writing**, which offers a very well established, structured, step by step approach to literature and composition.

Other English options we considered:

We also looked at such programs as **Hewitt Homeschooling: Lightning Literature & Composition , Lifepacs, Sonlight, Write@ Home, Brave Writer, Monarch, and SOS** and found them all to be strong, in our opinion.

SOCIAL STUDIES

We had a lot of flexibility for Social Studies, as our college choices gave us a long list of courses to choose from, and did not specify which of these courses we needed specifically. In fact, my teen was not required to do Social Studies each year. You may not have this same flexibility for social studies. It just depends on the college.

So we chose from a wide variety of subjects:

- World History
- US History
- Geography
- Economics
- Psychology
- Sociology
- Civics, etc.

We decided to use two of Oak Meadow's history courses, and also some geography from the Rainbow Resource catalog. Rainbow Resource Catalog and Site has tons of interesting options for homeschooling high school, and all the years before that as well. For U.S. History, we made our own course. For more information, see the *Resources for Buyers* page.

Then, senior year, we did a course in Government from *Northwest College*. That gave my daughter a dual credit course which showed the colleges that she could do college level work.

Other Social Studies options we considered:

We also checked out **SOS, Lifepacs, Tapestry of Grace and Sonlight**, all strong options.

FOREIGN LANGUAGE

Most colleges require two years of the same foreign language for their incoming freshmen. Some tier one or Ivy colleges ask for three or even 4.

Be sure to check with your colleges as to what languages they will accept.

Some colleges are now accepting American Sign Language, and almost all accept French, Spanish, German, Chinese, Japanese, Korean, etc. Some colleges do accept Latin, but there are others that only consider "living languages" and will not accept Latin.

We chose a Spanish 1 class from a regional school program in our area. It was offered three a week, and that gave our daughter wonderful, conversational in-person practice.

For Spanish 2, we went with the homeschool version of **Rosetta Stone (RS)** @ http://www.rosettastone.com.

I liked the homeschool version best because it included grammar, while the regular RS version did not. Also, our college choices preferred the homeschool version.

Other Foreign Language Options We Considered:

We also looked at **SOS**, and **Monarch,** but wanted something that focused more on conversational Spanish. Both of these courses did not.

There are so many options for foreign language. Cathy Duffy, cathyduffyreviews.com, has a number of reviews on foreign language curricula.

ONLINE HOMESCHOOL COURSES

Are you looking for online classes?

There are many educational companies that are offering specific online courses that are made for homeschoolers.

One of our favorites is the **Funda Funda Academy** (fundafundaacademy.com).

This online school provides full semester classes for homeschoolers including ones in the core subjects such as Chemistry and Geography. They also offer elective courses in Photography and other special interests. Learning is done through videos and projects, not worksheets and quizzes, making them meaningful and motivating for teens.

Are you looking for interactive, live online classes?

One of our favorite providers of live classes is the *Gifted Homeschoolers Forum* (https://ghflearners.org/ghf-classes/).

These classes give the students a classroom experience that is tailored to homeschoolers, especially those who are gifted or 2e (twice exceptional). They are set up so that each teen can link up with the teacher and the other teens online.

The GHF Classes are small to allow for lots of interaction, with a focus on adventurous learning and authentic projects. And building community.

Other online programs that we considered:

- **Seasons, LLC**
- **A Beka,**
- **Time 4 Learning**
- **Sonlight**
- **Monarch**
- **Easy Peasy**

FOR MORE INFORMATION: To get links for many of these homeschool curriculum resources, just copy and paste the link below to reach the *"Resources for Book Buyers Page"* in my blog.

LINK - https://www.bjshomeschool.com/2018/11/resource-page-for-book-buyers.html

Forms

Curriculum Planning Sheet – This is for sketching out ideas for curricula and resources one year at a time. Feel free to make extra copies of it for your use.

Chapter 6

Three Ways to High School Credit

What is a credit, anyway?

And when we get in the business of assigning credits to our kids, where will that lead us? Will we lose the very benefits that led us to homeschooling in the first place?

At first assigning high school credit seemed daunting to me. Would we have to finish every textbook, cover to cover, or calculate every quarter hour and record it on a form? And could we still make our own homemade courses for some subjects?

As homeschoolers, we look for signs of learning, and as we work with our kids 1:1 we know what they are getting and what they are missing.

Assigning credit is just a way to translate what your child has accomplished into terms that the outside world can understand.

Well, we found it to be a lot easier than we first thought. We could still assign credit and keep our nurturing homeschool style.

Below are three ways to approach high school credits. We used all of them. We needed to ramp up our recordkeeping, but still kept our nurturing, homeschool flavor.... well, most days, anyway!

1. THE TEXTBOOK METHOD

- When your child has been working in a textbook or online program for one year they have earned 1 credit.

- For an academic course (such as American Government) typically it would require one semester or one-half year to complete 1/2 credit.

Here's more on this from the Home School Legal Defense Association (**HSLDA**).

"If your child completes a high school-level text by a reputable publisher in an academic area (math, science, English, foreign language, or history), consider the material covered to be one credit. A one credit course typically requires one school year to complete."

It doesn't require that you check off every page, but that 75% or more has been covered.

"Covering the material in a textbook does not necessarily mean doing every problem, answering every question, or reading the book from cover to cover, but you should diligently cover the material presented. Some authors calculate teaching 75% of a textbook to equal one credit, but the bottom line is, don't shortchange your child." -------- HSLDA

This method of assigning credit can work just as well with an online course, from an established publisher, such as SOS, Tapestry of Grace, Oak Meadow, IEW, AmblesideOnline, or Time4Learning, etc.

We used this method for our Oak Meadow Literature and History courses, and also for our science and math. My teen worked for a year in each of these courses, but there was always room to focus more on one topic than another, and adapt it to her interests and needs.

But what about courses that are interest led or homemade?

2. THE HOURS METHOD

Here is a question that I often get - "What about homemade courses, such as homemade Literature courses, where your child reads their choice of classics, and writes essays about them that you have assigned?"

In this case, a rough calculation of hours spent can give you guidance in assigning credit. from HSLDA:

"For courses that do not use a standard high school-level textbook (perhaps you are putting together your own unit study, or you are using an integrated curriculum), log the hours that your child spends completing the course work. One credit is approximately 120-180 hours of work. The upper end of this range (180 hours) is usually appropriate for lab science courses, while 150 hours is the average for a yearlong academic course such as English or History."

They go on to say that this doesn't mean that you have to calculating every 15 minutes spent on the subject!

"Don't become legalistic in keeping track of each minute, but generally, when evaluating credit for an academic course, a good rule of thumb is 50 minutes a day, 5 days a week for 36 weeks, for a one-credit course. Logging hours is a good method of determining credit for elective courses such as art, music, sewing, carpentry, web page design, and homemade courses in core subjects, too." ----- HSLDA

So then, a half credit can be earned by working twice a week for approximately thirty-six weeks.

We used the "hours method" for these three homemade courses:

1. **Speech and Debate** - I kept a tally of hours in Youth and Government meetings, etc.

For example, my teen attended Youth and Government activities, which included public speaking practice and debate at their regular meetings and later at state wide meetings. We calculated a total of 90 hours, so this became a half credit course.

2. **Visual Art** - We did art project two times a week for a year, i.e. 36 weeks, which gave her one half credit.

3. **Photography** - We worked on this two or three times a week, going out with our cameras to do nature photography. I taught my daughter myself. It became a half credit course for fine arts credit....

What if my child demonstrates that they have learned something and we haven't counted the hours?

3. THE MASTERY METHOD

Whether your teen has mastered the concepts or skills over the course of a semester or even just during the high school years, credit can be awarded for mastery of that subject.

Take, for example, a homemade course in film production. My teen worked on a video, learning concepts and skills, made a video, and then entered it in a contest. It was accepted, and won. This indicated a beginning mastery in video production, so she earned a credit.

Say, your child wants to study drama. They sign up for a drama activity, gets a part, and participates in practices and a production. This shows a beginning level of mastery in drama, and could be a half or full credit based on the length of time spent in learning.

The mastery method could also apply to an apprenticeship. For example, you might award your child credit hours in based on working with someone skilled in, say, auto mechanics.

Once they show mastery, as determined by the skilled mechanic who is doing the teaching, they can receive high school credit for their work.

Assigning credit became something that my daughter looked forward to receiving. It was a tangible sign of all the work that she had accomplished.

*"College preparation doesn't have to be complicated. For homeschoolers, it is simply a series of planning stages that parents and students go through to make sure they are on the right track." ----LHSHS (*Let's Homeschool High School*)*

And it is possible to stay on your own homeschooling path. It just needs to be adapted for the process of "homeschooling towards college".... and you are on your own wondrous journey!

Forms

High School Credit Record Form – This form is designed for keeping track of the courses completed as they are finished, so you have a running tally of credits earned.

Homeschool Course Form – If you are making your own course, and are using the Hours Method of assigning credit, this form is for you.

Chapter 7

Making Your Teen's Transcripts

Homeschool transcripts are being accepted widely by colleges all around the U.S. Knowing what the college's want to see on your teen's homeschool transcript is key to getting into college.

Here are 10 key steps for doing your teen's transcripts AND showcasing your student to college admissions.

First, let's start with a definition of transcripts, from our friends at HSLDA:

"Transcripts are a record of the courses your child completed in high school, the credit he earned for each course, and each course's final grade. Transcripts also include personal information used for identification purposes and, usually, a grade point average (GPA)."

-- What to Include on the Transcript --

I recommend that your transcript to be just one page. That is what the colleges are used to seeing. The following should be included on the:

----------- Homeschool Transcript ----------

- School name and address, phone number
- Name of student, DOB
- ALL courses from 9th, 10th, 11th, and 12th grade years, with grades and credits earned (One-year study = 1 high school credit. One semester = 1/2 credit)
- Some colleges will accept work done in 8th grade also.
- Add in any community college courses, dual enrollment, any online courses, etc., as the homeschool transcript should include everything taken, so the college can see it all in one place.
- For those going to a 4-year college - Scores from SAT or ACT. Chose the *highest scores* and list them on your transcript.
- Student's graduation date and GPA - grade point average
- Parent signature with a date.

....compiled from HSLDA and Let's Homeschool High School.

What courses should be included on the transcript?

The homeschool transcript should include all the courses taken, at home and any outside courses, too.

Homeschool transcript serves as the clearinghouse for all of your teen's high school coursework. This allows college admissions officers to see everything, at a glance.

What about my homeschool's name?

-- Naming your Homeschool --

It is advisable to choose a name, like Johns Academy, instead of something like the Learning and Growing School, as it lends a more serious tone to your transcript.

What about activities, volunteering jobs, awards, etc.?

-- Awards and Activities --

Awards and activities are very important in showing your student's accomplishments and abilities. However, they don't go on the transcript unless your student has earned credit for them.

For example, we made a homemade course out of my daughter's speech and debate activities, so that went on her transcript. But her Irish dance activities, including awards and competitions did not.

You can list your teen's activities, leadership, awards, honor society, volunteer hours, or jobs held on the application itself. This is where we put her dance activities. Colleges like seeing each of their applicant's activities on the section dedicated for that on their application.

What should your homeschool transcript look like?

-- Sample Transcripts --

I liked looking at the samples. They got me started on the right track.

HSLDA Sample Transcripts

If you go to **HSLDA High School Transcripts**, scroll down to the Sample Transcript, then click Completed Transcript Example, you will find a number of samples to look at there.

I recommend keeping your transcript to one page. This is the format colleges are used to seeing.

What about calculating credits?

-- Calculating Credit --

Most colleges are looking for around 24 - 26 credits from their applicants. For high school courses, whether they are in your homeschool, at co-op, or online:

One year of study = 1 high school credit
One semester = 1/2 credit

Dual Credit Courses, such as those from a Community College are different as far as credits.

Dual Enrollment/College Level Courses

Generally, a one-semester 3-credit college course is equal to a year-long one-credit high school course.

One semester of dual credit = 1 high school credit

How do I figure the grade point average (GPA)?

-- Calculating the GPA--

Most colleges use the GPA to determine eligibility for an academic scholarship, along with SAT or ACT scores. The GPA is easy to calculate, and the colleges will be looking for it on each transcript. It is normally calculated using a 1-4 scale like this:

4 = A or A + = 4.33
3 = B or B + = 3.33
2 = C or C + = 2.33
1 = D or D + = 1.33

How to calculate GPA:

For example, your student earned a B, or a "3", in 1 credit course.
Multiply 3 x 1, i.e., the grade point value times the # of credits earned.
Do this same process for all of your teen's courses. Here's an example below:

Algebra A = 4.0 x 1 credit = 4.0
History B = 3.0 x 1 credit = 3.0
Biology B+ = 3.33 x 1 credit = 3.33
Spanish B = 3.0 x 1 credit = 3.0
Photography A = 4.0 x ½ credit = 2.0

Note - Do you see how the photography course came out as 2.0, because it was a one semester course?

Then add all the products together: 4 + 4 + 3 + 3.33 + 3 + 2 = 19.33

Then divide that #, 19.33, by the total number of credits earned: In the example above, the student earned 5 and ½ credits.
19.33 divided by 5.5 credits = 3.5

That gives you a GPA of 3.5, to be noted on the transcript.

What about AP or Honors courses?

--AP and Honors Courses--

If your student took an AP course, note that on the transcript with an asterisk * or something like that to make special note of it. Most colleges do not accept extra points added for honors courses, unless they were taken from an outside course. If it is an outside course, you can designate it on the transcript as well.

For the most part, I would recommend not using a weighted GPA, and identify the GPA as "not weighted" on the college application. It is also advisable to note your student's SAT or ACT score somewhere on the transcript as well. Pick the test with the highest overall score and note that one.

What if you just want a little help making your transcripts?

-- Frugal Resources for Transcripts --

Have you begun making your teen's transcripts, and found it to be a little daunting? Compiling all the necessary information and knowing what to put where can sometimes be overwhelming. When I worked on mine, I found that having help made all the difference.

I used Fast Transcripts myself, from HSLDA. They help with the record keeping, too. You can put each of your teen's courses in one at a time, and they will save them and compile the transcript for you.

Are there certain courses to be covered before graduation?

-- Graduation Requirements? --

As homeschoolers, we do not need to meet the public school graduation requirements. Let me say that again -- The state graduation requirements are set up for public school students, and as homeschoolers we are not bound to follow them. But it is important to check the homeschool law in your state, for any graduation requirements. In my state of WA, the parents decide when their student is ready to graduate.

But there are some states that DO have specific requirements for homeschool graduation, so it is advisable to check what your state requires at www.hslda.org/laws/Default.asp.

How can I show that my student is ready for college level work?

-- How can I show rigor? --

There are a number of ways to show rigor on the transcript. Pick and choose what works best for your student.

Add in an extra course in one or two of the required areas of study.

For example, my daughter did well in English, so we added an additional course in that area, which was Speech and Debate.

This was a homemade course, *but it showed rigor as it was additional to the requirements* in English in my daughter's college entrance requirements.

Add in a dual credit course or two, in your child's favorite subject. That shows that they are capable of college work.

Do an AP course, or an SAT Subject Test. Adding in more may be needed if you are looking at tier one colleges or Ivy universities.

Forms

See the **Sample Transcript** and **Fillable Homeschool Transcript Form** in the appendix.

Chapter 8

High School Electives and Activities

There is so much more to homeschooling high school than just core studies and meeting the college entrance requirements.

One of the top reasons that we homeschooled all the way was to foster our daughter's interests and grow her gifts.

Did you know that your teen's electives and activities can help them get into college?

Colleges are looking for self-motivated students with special interests and a desire to develop their talents. They want to see what activities and electives your student has completed when they apply to college. Whether it is in music, art, drama, web design, medieval history or Latin, colleges want kids who show initiative and perseverance.

Having the time for my teen to delve deeply into her interests is one of the reasons that we homeschooled all the way through high school. I encouraged my daughter to explore and try out different activities. Isn't that what homeschooling is about anyway?

Here are some of the ways to easily share electives and activities to college admissions...

Tips for Sharing Electives with the College

This can happen right on the application, through the homeschool transcript, or as part of the college essay. *Colleges want to see activities that your teen is really interested in, not just ones that one might think would look good on the college application.*

On the Application - There is a section for listing activities, volunteering, etc., right on the common application. It is easy to do, just fill in the blank.

On the Homeschool Transcript - Special interests can be made into elective courses, and listed on your teen's transcript. Not all activities need to be made into electives. They can just be listed on the application, as described above. The colleges are used to looking at the application for high school activities.

In the College Essay - There are essay questions to answer here, but the colleges also want to hear about your teen's unique interests and skills. Depending on the essay question that your student chooses, the college essay may be a place to share special interests as well. But make sure your teen answers the essay question they choose, without losing sight of what the prompt is asking.

Show Perseverance - Normally colleges just want to see the activities that are done in the high school years, but if your child has participated in a sport or other activity over a number of years, then go ahead mention all the years that they were involved. That's what we did for my teen's Irish dance.

My teen started Irish dance in 3rd grade, and then continued with it through high school. Therefore, we included all the years of her Irish dance on the application. You usually would not list your teen's elementary activities. *But this time it was important to include, as it showed two things that colleges look for - perseverance and a skill that has been well developed over time in an area of interest.*

Show Leadership - Any activity where your teen has been a leader counts, this includes church, helping in Sunday school, on a Teen Board, or volunteering at day camp.

Here are 7 high school activities that can help your teen develop skills in leadership:

Leadership Programs

1. Youth and Government – This program is a hands-on way to learn about state government, and gain speech and debate skills simultaneously. Youth meet in small groups, as student led delegations, then debate mock bills that they write. They learn legislative procedure and how a bill becomes a law, while also practicing public speaking and debate skills.

In the spring, all the delegations gather together to form a statewide *Youth Mock Legislature*. Students enact the roles of legislators and debate their mock bills with their peers. This program is available in 38 states across the country, and is sponsored by the YMCA. Students even elect their own youth governor each year!

2. TeenPack Leadership Schools – This is a well-established leadership program which provides groups and workshops that equip teens to become leaders in politics and society.

They offer state classes, four-day classes and a national convention, too. Their classes are held in 41 states at their state capitals. Many of my teen's homeschool friends participated in these events and learned a lot there. They looked forward to it every year.

3. Counselor-in-Training Programs – The Girl Scouts, Boy Scouts, and Camp Fire programs all offer counselor training to teens. Then they assist in summer day camps for younger kids.

4. Volunteering – Leadership skills can be developed through volunteering, *but we already knew that as homeschoolers.*

5. Parks Department Teen Board – Many parks departments have youth teen boards, who plan activities for younger kids, and that is a great way to learn leadership skills, too.

6. Police Explorers – Many police departments offer this program for youth ages 14-21. It includes lots of volunteer opportunities and leadership training as well. The program provides many volunteer opportunities and can help lead to a career in law enforcement.

7. National Christian Forensics Communication Association (NCFCA) – This is the longest standing nonprofit organization that offers speech and debate activities for homeschooled high schoolers. They meet locally in chapters, compete regionally, and hold a national championship yearly. Lots of my teen's homeschool friends participated in this, and loved it. They also hold short film and writing contests.

Making Your Own Electives

Most colleges ask for two or more electives, and they can be homemade, if you like. Here's one we did, video production. Just be sure to count the time spent doing online lessons, studying YouTube videos, writing the scripts and making the videos.

So many high school electives can easily be homemade.

If you are looking for more ideas for electives or activities for your teen, here is a list of 100 High School Electives and Activities that I have gathered for you to check out...

100 High School Electives and Activities

Animal Care – Help with family's animals, assist at the Humane Society, do an animal project 4H, compete at a state fair. This can easily be made into an elective.

Athletics – Are your teens interested in sports? Many Parks Department have leagues and classes, as does the YMCA, etc. Some public schools allow homeschoolers to join in their sports activities as well. – States that offer this option include Arizona, Colorado, Florida, Idaho, Iowa, Maine, North Dakota, Oregon, Utah, and Washington. For more information check with the HSLDA, Parks Department Leagues, YMCA, etc.

Archeology – Take a course at the community college or make your own.

Art – We took several classes from our Parks Department. The YMCA offers them as well. My friend's teen enjoyed Artistic Pursuits from Christian Books.

Art Appreciation

Automotive Repair

Bible Quiz – This program offers competitions at the district, regional and national levels in bible memorization skills. My daughter's friend competed locally, then had the honor of doing it on the national level and she enjoyed it very much.

Blogging – Set up a blog for your teen or have them set it up themselves. What a great way to get your teen writing!

Book Club – Attend your local library's club or make your own.

Boy Scouts – Earning badges, and progressing in Boy Scouts, such as achieving Eagle Scout, is a great activity for leadership development.

Business Management – This could include running an Esty shop, taking a course, or making your own.

Business Math

Career Exploration – This can be an elective for high school credit. Some ideas for this include interviewing family members and friends re their careers, doing online research into careers of interest, arranging to visit a site of interest.

7 Sisters offers a complete course in Career Exploration Curriculum Bundle, highly recommended.

Car repair – Learn alongside dad, help with car repairs, take a class, etc.

Carpentry

Ceramics – Our parks dept. offered great classes in ceramics, which my teen enjoyed.

Chalk Pastels Video Art Courses – Tricia Hodges is offering a variety of art courses in pastels, including two semester long courses, perfect for a solid art elective for your teen! Perfect for independent study. No need for a long list of supplies. Just get some construction paper and chalk pastels and you are ready!

Cheer – Cheer classes and or competitions, available through some Parks Departments.

Child Development – The 7 Sisters offer a complete course in Early Childhood Education. Assisting in a church nursery, babysitting, helping in a co-op class, or helping with younger siblings over time can all contribute to the learning.

Choir

Coding

College Planner – We made our own course in College Planner, which included college prep activities, ACT test prep, college visits, and more. All of these activities can count towards a high school credit and all of our colleges accepted them.

Comparative Religions

Computer Studies – Online, Programming, Web Design, etc. Making a website, and blogging can count as web design.

Composer Study

Cooking

CPR-First Aid

Crafting

Creative Writing – Why not take a creative writing break? We did this and it was one of my teen's favorite high school electives. I am a writer, so I taught my daughter the basics, then we made our own homemade course with NaNovWriMo.

Another way to go is to use *One Year Adventure Novel* or pick another resource such as *Learn to Write the Novel* from Christian Books. This can become an English credit. Creative writing is a great way to build up your teen's confidence in putting words on paper.

Dance – My daughter enjoyed studying Irish dance at a local dance studio for many years. There are many kinds of dance to consider, ballet, jazz, liturgical, etc. We started out with parks dept. classes in pre-ballet. What fun I had watching my little one learn to dance!

Desktop Publishing

Etsy Shop

Fashion

Financial Management

Fine Arts

Fitness Coaching

4H – They offer a variety of activities to develop kids and a teens' citizenship, leadership, responsibility and life skills. My daughter participated in their annual competitions at our state fair each year, and enjoyed photography, art, knitting, baking, and more. This gave her outside feedback on her projects, which was priceless.

Furniture Refinishing

Gardening – Building a veggie garden, studying gardening online, planning a flower garden, helping with garden maintenance at home can all count.

Geology

Girls Scouts

Graphic Design

Gymnastics – My daughter took lessons at our local gymnastics center. This was a great way for her to build strength and it also showed perseverance on the high school transcript, as she did this over a number of years. (Usually you would only include the high school activities on the college application.)

Hand Arts

Health

Home Economics – Cooking dinner once a week could become a ½ or full credit in home economics, depending on whether it was done for one semester or a year. Making a recipe notebook, trying out new recipes, etc.

Homeschool Scouts

Homeschool Sports Network – To find a homeschool sports program in your area, check out their **website**, which lists the states that offer sports around the country.

Horticulture

Interior Decorating

Jewelry Making

Journalism

Landscaping

Leadership – *See the list above.*

Life Skills

Marine Science

Marketing

Martial Arts – Many studios offer homeschool classes in martial arts.

Music – Music lessons, composer studies, playing in a band or orchestra, singing in a choir, performing, attending performances call all lead to a high school credit in music. Our area had a homeschool choir available.

Music Appreciation

Music Lessons

Nature Study

Nutrition

Oceanography

Office Skills

Orchestra

Painting

Photography – I taught my daughter photography, from age 8, and we did this together for many years and it later became a homemade elective. There are also online courses in photography and some parks departments offer classes as well.

Photo Shop

Physical Education

Plumbing

Programming

Psychology – 7 Sisters has a course in this, from a Christian perspective.

Research Skills

Robotics

Sailing

Sea Scouts

Sewing

Shakespeare

Sign Language

Social Media - Advertising

Sociology

Speech and Debate – National Christian Forensics Communication Association (NCFCA)

Speech 1 – *Public Speaking and Practical Life Skills* - by the 7 Sisters, Homeschool, also highly recommended.

Small Business

Stoa – Christian Homeschool Speech and Debate – This national organization offers Speech Events, Debate Events, and Tournaments

Theater and Drama – Take a class, usher at a drama production, join a local community theater group. My nephew participated in a homeschool drama program through his co-op.

Video Making – We made our own course in video-making, a true joy to do with my teen. It became a one-half credit elective on her homeschool transcript and was tons of FUN!

Voice Lessons

Volunteering – Such a great way to gain experience, build up confidence, leadership skills, and to try new things.

Some places to consider volunteering – Church youth activities, church nursery, the public library, nursery room at co-op, the Humane Society, Girl Scout or Boy Scout day camp, Parks department special needs programs, mission trips, nursing homes, church camps, day care or preschool, food bank, Y, YWCA, etc.

Above is a photo of my daughter helping a co-op class. She also tried her hand at volunteering at our local library. Most libraries around the country are set up for having teen volunteers. Some museums also offer volunteering. Volunteering can lead to a recommendation letter that can be sent along with your teen's college application.

Y (YMCA) – The Y has locations all over the U.S. and will give you a first-time guest pass.

Nothing like watching your teen as they discover and explore their special interests during the all-important teen years.

I loved doing electives with my daughter. But I followed her interests, and did not load on extra electives or activities just to show them to the colleges. Instead, we made time for her to develop her gifts and talents as it fit into our homeschool days and our family's schedule.

FOR MORE INFORMATION: To get links to many of these high school electives, just follow the link below to reach the Resources for Book Buyers Page.

LINK - https://www.bjshomeschool.com/2018/11/resource-page-for-book-buyers.html

Forms

Activities and Awards Form – This is just a handy place to list activities and awards that your student has done or received.

Homemade Course Form – If you want to create your own high school elective and use the Hours Method for assigning credit this form is for you.

Community Service Log – This is a place to record time spent volunteering. Colleges love to see volunteer experience on your teen's application.

Chapter 9

Making Your Own Homemade Courses

Our Video Production Course

One of the most fun benefits of homeschooling is that we can be as creative as we want to be. And that can include making your own courses.

We made a number of our own courses, which I will share. But of course, there are SO many ways to do this. I am sharing these just to give you ideas for your own courses.

We used a variety of quality homeschool curriculum in high school, but also enjoyed making some of our own courses.

We made courses including one in Creative Writing, another in Photography and then the three that I share here; U.S. History, Video-Making, and Speech and Debate.

OUR AMERICAN HISTORY COURSE

When it came time for our high school US History studies, we made our own course using a variety of sources. To do that, we picked a spine, then added a few more things, including geography, a primary source and some related art projects.

We started by picking a spine.

1. A Spine - My teen was a big part of choosing this resource, which served as a spine, i.e. a guide to follow and structure our course around. We chose *Short Lessons in US History* from Rainbow Resource catalog.

2. Geography - *U.S. History Map Activities*

This book is set up in a workbook style which my teen enjoyed, with comprehensive mapping activities for each major event in US History.

By answering the questions and mapping out each historical event, my daughter got a hands-on feel for what she had studied. And by writing about it and mapping it out, important historical events were easily memorized. We did not do every project in this book, just ones that were a good fit.

3. Primary Sources

We found a resource called ***The Patriot's History Reader*** by Dave Dougherty, Larry Schweikart, and Michael Allen. This book goes back to the original sources, including documents, speeches, and legal decisions that helped to shape our country. It was so convenient to have this at hand and it eliminated the need to search the internet for these.

4. Art

We used **American Landmarks** by Tricia Hodges, from *You Are An Artist*. She is a homeschool mom of 5 and a blogger.

My teen learned about our country's famous historical landmark while learning how to draw them with pastels. All that we needed was a set of chalk pastels.

The lessons introduce art principles using chalk art pastels. Tricia offers many more art courses including video-based options for all ages.

If you want to combine your American History course with English, here are some books that might be a good fit:

To Kill a Mockingbird
Uncle Tom's Cabin
The Federalist Papers
Tom Sawyer
Miracle at Philadelphia
Autobiography of Benjamin Franklin
Thomas Edison - from Heroes of History

Of course, if you add in American Literature, then you will be doing two high school credits; US History for one, and American Lit for another.

Here's one that we loved doing together...

OUR VIDEO MAKING COURSE

Making things, arts and crafts, and photography were always big in our house. One year my teen wanted to try her hand at filmmaking. This became a half-year long project worth ½ credit and offered many opportunities for creativity, such as:

- writing scripts
- story boarding
- planning shots
- finding friends to play as actors
- and then making videos.

This helped to balance out her core studies that year. She developed beginning skills in cinematography, filmmaking, and editing.

It was something that we shared on her transcript. Projects or clubs like this can show initiative organizational skills ability to the colleges.

Equipment and Software:

1. A video camera
2. Editing software - Pinnacle Studios 16
3. Tripod (or ask a friend to help with filming)

Resources for Video Making Course

1. *The Cutting Edge*

A documentary about film editing with, "clear explanations and clips from many groundbreaking videos."

2. *Behind the Scene Videos*

There are 26,000 behind the scenes videos, on Vimeo, where she learned about filming technique, sound production, lighting and set design.

3. *The Filmmaker's Handbook*

This book is a guide to producing, directing, shooting, and editing.

Assigning high school credit was easy, using the Mastery Method discussed in the chapter on High School Credits. By entering three films in filmmaking contests and getting them accepted there indicated a beginning level of mastery. She made three films and they all met the qualifications and rules for the contests.

This is just one way to make a filmmaking course. Yours may be totally different. Whatever way you do it, it can be one of your teen's fine arts credits, an elective credit.

OUR SPEECH AND DEBATE COURSE

Is your teen interested in leadership or speech and debate?

One resource we love is *Youth and Government*. Youth and Government is a Y sponsored activity that teaches teens about state government-hands on.

How do they do that?

Through yearlong activities that culminate in a Mock Youth Legislature event that is held in each state capital in the spring.

Teens meet weekly to write mock bills, based on how bills are made in the legislature. They also learn speech and debate skills.

Then teens gather from around the state, in an event, to act as Mock Legislators and vote to elect a Youth Governor.

This program offers great leadership experiences, training in speech and debate, etc., that can be listed on a college application.

My daughter's local delegation was full of homeschoolers, and most groups meet in their local Y's, who sponsor this activity. Youth and Government is offered in 38 states and Washington, D.C.

We made our course in Speech and Debate by just using *Youth and Government* activities.

Assigning high school credit was easy to do, just by using *the hours method* mentioned in Chapter 6. We just kept track of the time spent in meetings, debates, related homework, etc.

We used it for a Speech and Debate credit, but it could also have been a credit in State Government.

I hope this gives you ideas for what you and your teen want to put together. Many families continue with unschooling and use a very relaxed approach through the high school years, too.

You know your teen best.

FOR MORE INFORMATION: To get links to the resources mentioned visit:

RESOURCE PAGE FOR BOOK BUYERS

LINK - https://www.bjshomeschool.com/2018/11/resource-page-for-book-buyers.html

Chapter 10

Writing a Winning College Essay

Do the words *College Admissions Essay* make you cringe? They did for me. I was feeling more than a little nervous about this task and my teen was, too....

As it turned out, the essay was not nearly as hard as I thought it would be, and my daughter was able to write an essay that she could use for multiple college applications.

If your teen is using the Common Application, they will just have to write one essay. But if your prospective college has their own application or additional supplemental, then they will have their own essay prompts, different from the Common Application.

Whichever way you go this essay is a key component to the college application. But we all know that.

It serves as your student's introduction to the college, similar to what an interview would do.

But for many teens, writing about oneself can be very daunting. Like everything else related to college, we took it one step at a time.

Our 1st Step: Finding the Essay Prompts

We began by googling the Common Application, where we found the directions for their essay and the essay prompts. Some colleges use their own applications, which are unique to that college. If that is the case, their essay prompts will be listed on their own application.

Here are a few of the sample essay prompts from the Common Application, to give you an example.

NOTE – These prompts change each year. Be sure to look up the current prompts at www.commonapp.org.

Sample Essay Prompts (Not the current ones!)

1. **Some students have an interest, or talent that is so meaningful they believe their application would be incomplete without it. If this sounds like you, then please share your story.**
2. **Was there a hardship that you experienced in your growing up years? How did you work to overcome it?**
3. **Reflect on a time when you challenged a belief or idea. What prompted you to act? Would you make the same decision again?**
4. **Describe an event or activity that you did that you were perfectly comfortable doing, and why it felt like that, and why it was important to you.**

…. All well and good…. Once we had found our prompts, neither of us had any idea how to choose one!

We did know that the college essay was the best way for the college get to know our teen. So, to get things started, we made a list of the things that we wanted the colleges to know about her.

NOTE – This is the story of how I helped my teen prepare for her college essay...Your approach may be similar or very different.

Our 2nd Step – Brainstorming

Here's a question to answer - **What accomplishments, experiences, etc. can best describe your student to the college?**

To brainstorm, we just listed - leadership activities, and my teen's interests, such as dance, video-making, and photography. **We also thought of the things that would show perseverance, such as doing Irish dance over 8 years.** Then we listed her volunteer activities. Of course, every student's list, would be different.

We looked back at the essay prompts, and looked for a prompt that might relate to something on our list.

Our 3rd Step – Choosing the ESSAY Prompt

Here's some advice from some experts. Nancy Burgoyne, from *Fat Envelope Essays* says:

"Choose a topic that allows your student to shine. Think of the essay as kind of an interview with college admissions. Pick whichever prompt will help the college to get to know your teen better. "

"Decide which topic has the most potential; it should be something that you feel strongly about so that it really comes alive when you write about it." ...from 11 Tips for Writing the College Essay, by the American School Counselor Association

"Write about common topics, real experiences that your teen has had and how they were meaningful to them. Avoid being too creative or controversial." ... from Nancy Burgoyne, of *Fat Envelope Essays*

She also wanted to share about her leadership activities, which she could write about it essay prompt #1.

We both also thought about prompt #2, where she could share her experiences overcoming some visual issues.

We had three options, and my teen couldn't decide. So we took off, and headed for the beach.

Sometimes inspiration comes more from the breaks that we take, than from thinking about it....

By spending time out in nature, somewhere in those beautiful waves, my daughter found the answer to her essay......and chose her essay prompt.

My teen decided to write about her youth conference, an event that had personal meaning for her, **and something that she was passionate about.** She chose essay prompt #4....

Which essay prompt sparks interest in your teen? What are they passionate about?

NOTE - If you are writing about hardships, I recommend focusing on the positives not the difficulties. Speak to how they were overcome. This shows the college your student's problem-solving skills, motivation, and resilience.

Our 4th Step – Outlining and Writing

The next day, my teen sat down and began her first draft using her initial ideas. It was important that she not just write about what happened at her youth conference, *but also how it affected her personally.*

"Don't just recount, reflect. When recalling events, you need more than a play by play. Describe what you learned from the experience and how it changed you." Princeton Review – The College Essay.

She sketched out an outline for her essay, choose her main points, and then began working on her opening paragraph. With this outline in hand, she worked on her draft for a few days, then let it sit.

When she got it out again, it was fresh, and she reworked it into a second draft. Taking some time off was helpful, as it gave her time to ponder and rework phrases. This helped her to share herself in a more authentic way. Once the essay was written, it was time for revisions.

Our 5th Step - Revisions

Next, my teen looked at her essay again to check and see if it followed the principles of a well-structured essay. *The colleges will all look for that.*

Reviewing the structure of a good essay, such as from IEW, or Oak Meadow or from Time for Learning helped a lot. Reviewing things like the structure, topic sentences, paragraph writing, etc., helped my teen to revise and restructure her essay, which was key. So look at the first draft with your teen, and ask them to revise it as needed.

"A good essay will generally deal with a single incident or a small part of your experience. Don't try to cram everything in. Additionally, since you are limited on space, you should avoid listing your accomplishments. These things will appear on your transcript and in other parts of the application." ......from Homeschool World - Your College Admissions Essay by Austin Web.

Then it was time for editing.

Our 6th Step – Editing

Reading the essay over multiple times was key. In addition, it is nice to have an outside person to check the essay for editing purposes. It is important that this essay be written by the student, of course, but many essay tutoring services recommend having another person read it over for editing.

Our cat decided to help, all the way......

Grammar, Spelling, Punctuation, and the Organization of the Essay are crucial.

So that's how we went about tackling the college essay. And, boy, did it feel good when it was submitted! Lastly, I leave you with 3 tips for writing the college essay from HSLDA:

1. Choose a topic that will highlight you.

2. Keep your focus narrow and personal.

3. Show, don't tell.

Forms

Writing the Personal Essay – Here is a list of steps for your teen to go through for writing their personal essay. It can serve as a checklist or reminder of the steps to follow, to be sure not to leave any of them out.

Chapter 11

Course Descriptions and Reference Letters

Homeschool transcripts are being well accepted by colleges, especially when two important things come along for the ride - course descriptions and reference letters.

Course descriptions and reference letters help to showcase your child's accomplishments to the colleges.

COURSE DESCRIPTIONS

The good news is that not all colleges ask for course descriptions. But if your college does, I found that they weren't really hard to do. Let's start with a definition.

1. What is a course description?

"Course descriptions provide the details of the course and usually include a list of the materials used... grading method, and evaluation of credit. You are the one to decide how detailed your course descriptions will be." – HSLDA

2. What should I include in them?

The purpose of course descriptions is to let the colleges know what was done in your teen's courses, and to what extent or depth.

Here's 4 things to include in your course descriptions:

- What are your expectations for the course, i.e., what do you expect your student to do?
- What materials will you be using?
- How will the grade be determined?
- How much credit will be earned?

Here's a sample of how I wrote a course description:

This 1 credit course will cover US History, from 1659 - present. The student will learn key U.S. History facts and will read _____ books, will write _____ research papers, will participate in an historical reenactment, and will complete unit studies on chosen US history topics. The grade will be based on written reports, essay tests, and daily assignments.

3. Should I list all of the materials that we used?

Your list of materials can be a summary of what you used and does not need to include every detail. The course description summarizes what you did, so it does not need to be a whole course syllabus. In fact, longer descriptions are less likely to be read. Therefore, I suggest aiming for a paragraph in length. But as the parent you decide how to do it.

The materials that you use can include a wide variety of learning resources, such as texts, DVD's, websites, unit studies, field trips, related community activities, living literature, free reading books, projects completed, internet research, etc.

4. Can I use the course summary that comes along with the textbook?

If you are using textbooks, feel free to use the summary or description of the course from the homeschool catalog or website. When using a textbook, HSLDA recommends including the authors, publishers, and date of publication for each text.

5. Don't confuse the transcript with the course descriptions.

As you know, the transcript is a one-page document that lists all of your teen's high school courses, with the grades, and credits earned. Course descriptions, on the other hand, describe what has been done during each course in detail.

They are written in a separate document, and are sent to the colleges along with the transcript and the college application.

6. What about record keeping?

Keeping records of textbooks, living literature, etc., early on, can be such a help in making your descriptions. I just jotted down what I thought we would be doing and working on, and then revised it at the end of the year. With these notes, it was so much easier for me to do our course descriptions.

Please see "Forms" at the end of this chapter, for a record keeping form, if you would like a form for your record keeping.

Along with course descriptions, reference letters can also be key to your teen getting into college.

COLLEGE REFERENCE LETTERS

Reference Letters can be fun to do and are a big help in getting your teen into college. They give admissions officers a way to get to know your student from the perspective of other adults in their life.

If your student is taking an online course, or at a college or community college, then your teen already has a teacher to ask for a reference. But many homeschoolers don't have one available, nor do they have a school counselor to ask. Therefore, letters from your student's activities can be just the ticket.

College reference letters can come from any adult who knows your student well. It can be from a teacher, a coach, a mentor, a dance instructor, a minister, etc... Really from any adult who can speak to your teen's character and abilities. The colleges want to know if your teen has the capability to succeed in college, and these leaders can speak to that.

When my teen applied to college, we used letters from the teachers of her Youth and Government, Irish dance, and volunteer activities.

These references were accepted by the colleges that my teen applied to and helped her get accepted. Colleges are getting used to seeing a variety of sources for the reference letters.

Look around for the most important adults in your teen's life, and help your teen ask them for a college reference letter.

When my teen requested letters of reference, the activity leaders were happy to help. But sometimes it's nice to request these references in writing.

Reference Letters and the Common Application

The Common Application also has some specific requirements for homeschooled applicants related to reference letters. As homeschoolers, we are to do a special document for our teen's Common Application: the Counselor Recommendation Letter.

This recommendation is to be written by you, the homeschool parent. It is required if you use the Common Application but it is not hard to do. *More on that is in the next chapter.*

Whether you use the Common Application or not, it is important to ALSO send a number of reference letters to the colleges.

Of course, they love hearing from teachers, but that is not required. In addition to that, it is also helpful to submit reference letters from your teen's high school leaders, such as coaches, co-op teachers, coaches, etc.

As mentioned, often the leaders and teachers at co-op know our kids well, and they can be a great source for our reference letters.

Requesting Reference Letters

When my teen requested letters of reference, the activity leaders were happy to help. But sometimes we found that it was nice to request these references in writing.

I put together a form that your teen can use to request college reference letters, and that is available in the appendix. This form can make it easier for your teen to make their reference request, but just handing the letter to their high school leader or coach.

It also gives the activity leader a bit of a guide as to what to write in their reference letter, as that information is included in the form.

But be sure to include other college references letters from their coaches, co-op teachers, youth ministers, etc as discussed above. Their letters can be a real asset to your teen's college application. These extra reference letters are key to getting your teen into college and will allow admissions to get to know your teen well.

For Support

There is an email group called **hs2coll@yahoogroups.com** where family's share their experiences with going from high school @ home to college. They discuss using multiple recommendation letters for their college applications, along with other tips for aiming towards college. This group is especially helpful if you are aiming towards Ivy's.

Forms

Course Descriptions Record Keeping Form - This is a place for recording keeping... to keep track of what you did for each course, making your course descriptions easier, at the end of the year.

Reference Letter Request Form – Print and fill in the blanks! Your teen can use this form to send to their activity leaders or instructors, as a way to request a reference letter.

Chapter 12

The Common Application

The Counselor Recommendation Letter and more.

Applying to college can seem so daunting. Even knowing which college application form to use can be an issue. Some colleges use their own application forms, which can simply be found on their website.

Then there is the **Common Application**.

Using the Common Application has many advantages.

It has it's own site and many 1,000's of colleges are now using this application form. If your teen's colleges are on their list, then you only have ONE application form to fill out. Once it is completed, your teen's Common Application will be sent to all the colleges that they choose.

That can be so convenient, with only one place to upload your teen's transcripts. At the same time, there are special things to know about when using the Common Application as a homeschooler.

I am sure that you have you heard the terms - School Profile? or the Recommender Account?

What's the School Report about for a homeschooler? *And did you know that now we have to write the counselor letter for our student?*

If your student is homeschooled, we are required to write their counselor letter for the Common Application.

The opportunity to serve as your student's counselor reference can be seen as a positive. The colleges want to hear from you, the homeschool parent.

I put together a step by step approach for dealing with all of these things in the Common Application.

BJ's Guide to the Common Application

It includes:

- Getting Started
- The Recommender Account
- The School Report
- The Counselor Letter
- The Teacher Evaluation
- Resources for Support
- For More Information

Before we get into the details of the Common Application, let's recall that the colleges are becoming more and more homeschool friendly. There are some colleges that are actively seeking out homeschooled applicants, who are often very self-motivated, and an asset to campuses.

GETTING STARTED WITH THE COMMON APPLICATION

1. Ask your student to make their account on the Common Application Website.

When they do that, they can list their prospective colleges. Fill out **Profile** and **Family** sections. You'll see them as you go along. Easy.

2. Next, look for the section called **Education** and click on "Find School". A window will pop up that lists schools in the area.

Scroll down to the bottom of that list and click "Homeschooled." Click "Graduated" or will graduate. Be sure to do that.

3. Next the site will ask for the Counselor's name. Since your student was homeschooled, the counselor will be you.

Your teen will then enter YOUR contact information in the spaces asking for the "Counselor". You, the homeschool educator, will be listed as the counselor, as that is how the Common Application wants to do it.

4. **That will trigger an email to be sent to you, the homeschooling parent.** This email will instruct you how to set up your **Recommender Account.**

That is where you will be doing two important things, the SCHOOL REPORT and the COUNSELOR LETTER. Both are discussed below. *For now, just save that email.*

Your teen will continue to fill out their sections of the Common Application. An important part for them will be the *Activities List.* This section is for listing activities, such as volunteering, part time work, church youth group, 4H, etc.

Meanwhile, you will want to continue filling out the application as follows:

5. You as the parent will be answering the questions on your Common Application that pertain to your "school", i.e., homeschool. These are just basic questions about your homeschool, and many of them will not pertain, so feel free to use N/A on those.

This is not complicated to do.

It is just a matter of following along and answering the questions. This is the place to report facts about your homeschool, like what GPA scale you used, and how many honors or AP course were offered, if any, etc. You can mention any public school or colleges that your student attended part time, if they did.

(The colleges know that some of the questions in this section make no sense for homeschooled applicants.) But be sure to put N/A, and not skip any questions.

Your student will need to continue filling out the rest of the application, including listing their activities and extra-curriculars, when asked to do so.

Now, please go find the email that was sent to you, the "counselor".

Remember, this is the email we mentioned in step #4. This will give you instructions for setting up your Recommender Account.

That is the next important step.

WHAT IS THE RECOMMENDER ACCOUNT?

Since 2015, the colleges now want to hear from you, the homeschool parent, via what they call the **Recommender Account.**

They want to hear more about your homeschool and your student from you. Here is how to get started:

Follow the instructions in the email that was triggered by your student as explained above. It will guide you to set up the **"Recommender Account".**

This account will lead you to start your Recommender work and has three sections:

- Profile - Identifying information
- Students - Connecting with your student
- Workspace - That's where you do the Counselor Letter, etc.

For the Profile - Just answer as best you can. Create a name for your homeschool, such as "Smith Academy", and follow along with the questions listed. Many will be N/A, like class ranking, as we don't have that as a homeschoolers of course.

The Students Section - Search for your student by name and answer the questions. *The Common App Ready* section explains much more on how to do these first sections and more.

Work Space Section -

Here you will be doing the two most important things...

- The School Report
- The Counselor Recommendation

This sounds daunting, but both of these will help the colleges get to know your student, from you, the one who knows them best. Here's some help for both of these documents.

Let's look first at...

THE SCHOOL REPORT

For this section - Answer the questions one at a time and upload your own description of your homeschool if you don't have enough room.

HOMESCHOOL - *"Please provide any information about the applicant's homeschool experience and environment that you believe would be helpful to the reader, e.g. educational philosophy, motivation for homeschooling, instruction setting, etc."*

They ask about your grading scale and/or how you evaluate your student's learning.

There is also a section on any outside courses taken, such as at a community college, etc. Fill in the information on each of the classes that your student did OUTSIDE of the home. If they didn't do any, just indicate that.

You may add more comments on how you did your grading and expand on your homeschool philosophy, etc.

Next Step - Uploading

In the School Report section, you will also:

- Upload your teen's transcript
- Upload your course descriptions

Add them only a few pages at a time, as that is what is recommended to avoid tech issues on their site.

Now, let's turn to...

THE COUNSELOR LETTER

As the parent, you will fill out this form as the Counselor for your teen. You have to act as the counselor and do the Counselor Letter Recommendation. You can't have someone else do it. That's the rule.

The same person who filled out the School Report does the Counselor Letter. And that's you. But that's ok....

It is not hard to do.

The colleges want to hear from you, and that is a good thing, as you know your student best. Here's how to get started:

Now you have the chance to share about your student directly to the colleges.

You will be asked - how long you have known the student, context, words to describe student. Then it asks you to upload your Letter of Recommendation document OR Provide a short evaluation (1000 words or less).

Here is the prompt describing the Letter of Recommendation.

"Please provide comments that will help us differentiate this student from others (max. 1000 words). We especially welcome a broad-based assessment and encourage you to consider describing or addressing - academic, extracurricular and personal characteristics."

Lee Binz, (from www.homehighschoolhelp.com) gives this advice on your Counselor Letter here:

"The counselor letter should include a header and salutation, your signature and title. You can give your title as Guidance Counselor, Homes Educator, or Homeschool Parent. It should include enough information about the student to fill a page or two.... not longer. Your goal is to make the letter short and clear."

"Don't write about what the student did NOT do, but focus on what they DID do.... This is a letter about what was done, written in the most positive light possible... Write only about high school, with no mention of grade school or junior high. Be professional, ensure it is perfectly edited..." from Lee Binz, *The Home Scholar*

If you feel uncomfortable dealing with the Counselor Letter, some of my friends have called the Admissions Office of your likely colleges and asked them for guidance.

Did you know that the colleges often employ students to answer the phone in Admissions? So, it is not daunting. Ask for a supervisor if needed.

Ask them directly what they want to see in the School Profile and the Counselor Recommendation Letter. I encourage you to do that, as Admissions really does want to help good students get accepted.

You can have someone else who knows your student well support what you said in your counselor letter. I even have a form to use to invite others to become a college reference for your student. That can be found in the appendix and is downloadable.

There is one more requirement to consider.

THE TEACHER EVALUATION

An **academic reference** is required as well. It is called the **Teacher Evaluation**.

What do we as homeschoolers do about that?

It is preferable to have this come from a teacher of sorts. You can ask a co-op teacher, tutor, online instructor, or other adult who has been involved in helping to teach your teen for one of these.

Of course, using a college professor from a dual credit course, or a professor from a community college would work very well, too. But that is NOT required.

Chapter 13

Preparing Your Teen for College Writing

We all know that good writing skills are important to success in college. No matter what major your student will be doing, they will be faced with a lot of writing assignments.

I was nervous when my teen first started college. Would she be able to handle the writing that was required? Well, I found out that I needn't have worried. My teen did exceedingly well on the freshman writing assignments. Her first essays were even asked to be used as examples for the rest of the class by her professor. Hooray for Homeschooling! Looking back, here are 7 things that were key to preparing my daughter for college writing:

1. First Thing - Write A Lot

I encouraged my daughter to write. A lot!…. And in whatever way she felt motivated to do it. Here are a few projects that she enjoyed, when she was feeling reluctant to write….

1. Write about an interesting newspaper article.
2. Rewrite the dialog in a favorite short story
3. Write how to articles - such as a recipe, or how to find a good deal on cell phones, etc.

It is important to have your teen also learn to write different types of essays, such as narratives, expository essays, persuasive essays, compare and contrast essays, etc.

Write@Home, Brave Writer, IEW, and Oak Meadow are all solid resources for high school writing.

2. Read A Lot

Whether you use a prepared curriculum, like **IEW, Oak Meadow, SOS**, or put together your own course, studying literature is vital for college preparation. Many colleges ask for both literature and composition for each year of high school English. Our colleges asked for just 3 years of literature and comp.

Doing your own homemade courses can work well, too. By choosing good literature and just assigning essays to go with it. Time4Learning has a helpful resource for do-it-yourselfers. Free reading is great, too, and our colleges were happy to see that our daughter read a variety of books and were not only classic literature.

3. Do Literary Analysis

Studying literary analysis was helpful for my daughter. It helped to develop the critical thinking skills that she would later need in college. Many of the prepared English programs, mentioned above, will guide you in teaching this important skill.

Oak Meadow, did a great job of teaching literary analysis to our daughter. They began by asking lots of questions for her to ponder like plot, setting, character development, etc. These questions helped her to really dive into literary analysis. Ambleside Online also has a great sample list of narration questions. Another great resource on this is from IEW – Windows to the World – An Introduction to Literary Analysis.

4. Spend Time Discussing Literature with your Teen

Discussions were also key to my teen's understanding of literary analysis. After she answered the critical thinking questions in her Oak Meadow course, we would sit down and discuss each of them together.

Oak Meadow's teacher's manual was very helpful in guiding our discussions. It helped me to lead discussion on the why's and how's of the story, character development, and how the setting impacted the plot. I have great memories of doing this with my daughter.

5. Creative Writing

If your teen is interested in creative writing, I would encourage them to practice it. Creative writing is a great way for kids to learn the components of literature - setting, point of view, characters, plot, etc. It also is a great confidence builder for later essay writing.

6. Do Research Reports

Writing research reports was also important. That gave my daughter practice in the all the components of researching, which was just what she needed in her freshman year in college. She also learned good note taking skills, along with how to compile her data, build an outline, and do the all-important bibliography.

7 Sisters Homeschool has a course in research report writing and ones in essay writing that I recommend.

To make learning these skills FUN we set up each writing assignment to be teen led. My daughter chose many of the topics that she researched during her high school years. (And she appreciated that once she got to college and no longer got to choose her topics!)

7. Practice the Steps of Writing - from Brainstorming to Publishing.

Time4Learning has a simple outline of the steps of writing.

It lists the steps of the writing process:

- Prewriting
- Outlining
- Drafting
- Revising
- Editing
- Publishing. Learning how to make and follow an outline can really be useful.

For extra help for incoming freshmen, many colleges also offer summer classes in composition, too.

Chapter 14

Dealing with College Testing
SAT/ACT

Does the thought of having your teen take the SAT or the ACT give you pause?

All of the colleges on my daughter's list required either the SAT or the ACT.

It is so nice to see that some colleges in our area are dropping the SAT/ACT requirements. But most colleges in the U.S. still require and rely on them to determine student ability, although there are some new college entrance tests that are getting started to be used. For the most part, however, colleges are still requiring the SAT or the ACT.

Did you know that the SAT/ACT along with your student's GPA are the two most important factors in getting scholarships?

The SAT

The SAT is a college entrance test that is set on a scale of 400–1600. It consists of two big sections, Reading and Writing, and Math. There is also an optional essay section. It does not itself cover science, but some of the reading passages may include that subject.

Since test scores are so important, we began thinking about test prep starting in 9th grade. You do not have to start that soon. It depends on each family's needs.

Preparing For the SAT
– In 9th Grade –

We started adding in tests and quizzes, just for practice, during her 7th, 8th, and 9th grades years. It was easy to do, by choosing curricula that offered some testing along with it, such as *Switched-On-Schoolhouse*.

This practice helped to build confidence for later SAT testing. We made sure that she had practice with testing not only in math, but also in the softer subjects, like Social Studies and English. If you haven't done this ahead of time, there is always time to build that in now.

Once she had built up her confidence in test taking skills, she was ready to try her hand at the PSAT...

Taking the PSAT
– In 10th or 11th Grade –

We did the PSAT in 10th grade. Why? Again, it was for practice. Most families do the PSAT in 11th grade, when it counts for the Merit Scholarship awards. But we did it in both grades. And for us, the practice was worth it. You know your student, and of course, we all know that each one is different and has unique needs.

The PSAT is usually given in public schools, in October, only once a year. To schedule taking the test, we called our local public school. We did that in early September to be sure that we could get it all arranged.

Our next step was to decide when to take the SAT itself...

Scheduling the SAT
– 11th Grade is recommended –

The SAT is offered 6 to 8 times a year. It is helpful to have had Geometry and Algebra 2 before taking the SAT. We decided to aim for taking the SAT during spring of 11th grade. Some families do it earlier.

We began studying for the SAT during the previous winter quarter. Why do SAT prep? Even if your student is rockin' it in English and Math, they are sure to encounter different types of questions on the SAT test itself. The questions vary a lot from what they would see in their high school courses.

SAT prep is so valuable as it helps your teen learn how the test works, and become familiar with what the questions will look like. We made time for prep every day, did the *SAT Questions of the Day*, and worked through multiple test prep books prior to her test date.

After her first SAT test, we considered whether to go ahead or do the SAT again...

Take the SAT again?

This is a question that often comes up re college testing. Is it really necessary to take the test again, to try raising up the scores?

I see two considerations here, for retesting.... or not. First, looking at the scores, do they reflect your student's abilities? If yes, then why retest? If you think that the scores are really lower than your student's ability, then it may make sense to test again.

The other factor in play is the specific college or colleges that your student is considering. If you wonder what a specific college is looking for, regarding test scores, it is not hard to find out. Each of our colleges had the average SAT scores of incoming freshmen on their websites.

Just an aside - Re-testing just to get into a prestigious college may not be a good idea. If a student has prepared and the scores seem to reflect their abilities, then maybe it is not the best idea to re-test.

If a student gets into a college that they really are not ready for, based on high scores from multiple re-tests, then they may end up where they were not meant to be. That it might, after all, not be a good fit.

For us, we set up a more formal SAT prep regimen, even making it into it's own course. We called it **College Planner** and assigned it one/half credit. This credit was accepted by our colleges.

Now that we have looked at early preparations, the PSAT, when to schedule the SAT, and whether to test again, let's pause for a moment.

(Also key to the whole SAT thing is to get a cat or dog, if you don't have one. Our cat was a super and patient study buddy for my high schooler, lol!)

For me, the most important thing to consider with the SAT, and really everything about homeschooling, is that each child/teen is different, and has unique needs.

Isn't that why we chose to homeschool?

There are ways to get accommodations from the College Board for the SAT/ACT, involving a lot of steps to follow. I refer you to that College Board for that. Some students with disabilities are granted extra time for testing and/or other accommodations.

The ACT Test

The ACT test is another choice for college entrance testing.

What is the different between the ACT and the SAT?

The ACT is more of an achievement test, while the SAT is more of aptitude test.

Does my teen need to take both tests?

I have never seen a situation where the student needed to take both tests.

The ACT Test

The ACT test is set on a scale of 1-36. It covers English, math, reading and science reasoning. It also has an optional essay. The science section tests critical thinking skills, not knowledge of science-specific materials.

Many families chose the ACT as they feel it is a better fit for their homeschooled teens.

The choice is yours. Most colleges ask for either the ACT or the SAT, although a few other test options are being offered lately, too, by some colleges.

TEST PREP SAT/ACT Resources

Just click the link below to get our list of SAT and ACT Prep Resources.

Some are free and many are frugal. There are many ACT resources available for ACT prep, but since we chose to do the SAT, our list mostly focuses on that.

To reach a list of SAT/ACT Resources - Just put this link into your search bar and it will take you to this document, Resources for Book Buyers.

LINK - https://www.bjshomeschool.com/2018/11/resource-page-for-book-buyers.html

Chapter 15

There are many different strategies that families use to pay for college. And as a parent of a college grad, I know we need every bit of help that we can get. For sure.

Of course, the best way is to somehow qualify for a full ride from the college itself. But as you know, these monies are getting smaller and harder to qualify and earn.

When our daughter was headed to college, we used a variety of search methods to find scholarship money for our daughter. But most of the help came directly from the college itself, in the form of Merit Aid.

Did you know that most of the college scholarship money comes directly from the colleges?

MERIT AID FROM THE COLLEGES

The highest number of scholarships are awarded by the colleges and they are based on:

- ACT or SAT scores or sometimes alternate tests
- GPA

Colleges will look at test scores and the GPA on your teen's homeschool transcript. That is where we got the most help for our teen.

If your student's test scores do not reflect their true abilities, consider re-testing and doing more SAT or ACT prep.

Lessa Scherrer from College Inside Track recommends:

"Apply to colleges where your test scores and GPA are in the top 25% of the admitted class so you will get merit money."

This approach recommended by a certified college counselor, can be key to getting a scholarship directly from the college.

Did you know that most colleges ask you to do the FAFSA when even just applying for merit aid?

The FAFSA

The *FAFSA* is the *Free Application for Federal Student Aid.* It is recommended that you do the FAFSA even if you do not qualify for financial assistance.

Most colleges require their prospective students to have the FAFSA filed, as they pull names from that for merit aid. It comes out in October each year. So when your student is a senior in high school, be sure to do this form.

Tips for Doing the FAFSA:

- Use info from your tax return the year before
  or
  connect your tax return to the FAFSA.

  Directions for this are on the FAFSA form online.

- Write down your user ID and password for future reference.

- To see what kinds of questions are included, go to the FAFSA4caster.

This is key: Do the FAFSA as early as possible., as Merit Aid is given out on a first come, first serve basis.

Another top source for college scholarships is the National Merit Scholarship Program.

NATIONAL MERIT SCHOLARSHIPS

You probably have heard of the *National Merit Scholarship Program.* To qualify, your teen needs to take the PSAT in the fall of junior year. Awards are based on their test scores.

The next place to find college scholarships are in local, state, or national outside scholarships programs.

OUTSIDE SCHOLARSHIPS

Other scholarships do not have as much money available as the first two options that we discussed. They also tend to be smaller and only last one year, but they can still be a help.

Search for local or state scholarships in your area. The number of applicants will be smaller. Local scholarships can be a better source as less applicants will be involved. State scholarships are better sources than national ones for the same reason.

The more that the scholarship requires of the applicant, the higher chance of winning one.

There are many smaller scholarships that require writing a speech or giving an essay, such as those offered by:

- SAR - Youth Contests and Awards -
LINK - https://www.sar.org/education/youth-contests-and-awards

- DAR - National Scholarships -
LINK - https://www.dar.org/national.../scholarships/general-info

- VFW - Youth Scholarships -
LINK - https://www.vfw.org/community/youth-and-education/youth-scholarships

WHERE TO SEARCH FOR OUTSIDE SCHOLARSHIPS

This is by far not an extensive list, but here are our favorite places for outside scholarships:

1. **Scholarships.com** has a Search Directory of over 3 million dollars in scholarships.
LINK - https://www.scholarships.com/

2. **FastWeb** is another large popular site. LINK - https://www.fastweb.com/

3. **The College Board** has a **Scholarship Search** section, including over 6 billion in scholarship money. LINK - https://bigfuture.collegeboard.org/scholarship-search

4. **The College Board** also has a new program called **Opportunity Scholarships**
LINK - https://opportunity.collegeboard.org/

5. **24 Great Scholarships for Homeschooled Students**
LINK - https://www.top10onlinecolleges.org/scholarships-for/home-schooled-students/

One last idea for money saving --- Have you thought of focusing on commuter colleges that are nearby?

DUAL CREDIT

Of course, enrolling in dual credit programs can save a lot of money.

Many families go that route, as well as doing AP courses to get college credit, or CLEP exams. But will the college that your teen goes to accept theses college credits?

The best thing to do with those approaches is to first check with prospective colleges.

Dual credit earned in high school may not be accepted fully or even at all at a prospective university. Unfortunately, this is true in many cases.

Some colleges even want their college major prerequisites to be done on their campus instead of before. In those cases, the college will not accept dual credit.

Researching this ahead of time can prevent wasted effort and give peace of mind. There are many colleges that do accept dual credit, but it is helpful to find out about this beforehand.

Earning an Associate's degree with a direct transfer from the community college to the 4-year college is another great way to go. That route was provided by many of the local community colleges in my state of Washington.

Another path we considered to save on our college costs was to apply to the colleges within commuting distance from our home. We did this and it ended up saving us 50% in college costs.

College funding can be a big hurdle, but the rewards of a good college education for our teens make it all so worth it.

Chapter 16

Dealing with "Those" Questions from Others

Knocking on a college's door can seem so daunting, especially as a homeschooler. Do you ever hear these kinds of questions from family or friends?

- Will your teen be ready for college level work?

- Will they be able to compete with other students, whether from public or private schools?

We heard these kinds of questions during the high school years at home. But after seeing our daughter do well in her first quarter of college, those questions all but disappeared.

Our daughter, like so many homeschool grads, did well in college. She earned her degree in Communications, following her special interests developed during high school.

Some colleges even recruit homeschooled applicants. They want those self-motivated teens who know how to find the answers to their questions and know where to look.

And do so independently.

We found that homeschooling prepared our teen very well for college. Here's 7 ways it did. Feel free to use any of these when asked questions by homeschool doubters.

1. Homeschooling can best meet teen's individual learning needs.

Homeschooling created an environment that nurtured and prepared our daughter well for college. It gave us the flexibility to not only challenge her intellectually, but also explore and find ways to accommodate for her learning issues during the early years, similar to ADHD.

If she had been in public or private school, she would have been faced with learning most everything through listening to the teacher, in front of the class. That would not have worked for our daughter. And if she was tested, with only verbal directions, she would have struggled. In homeschooling, we used visual and tactile (hands-on) approaches, and she loved learning and excelled in it.

As a homeschooler, she was able to learn in the way that she liked best. That is just the tip of the iceberg...

2. Homeschooling builds confidence by providing a strong foundation, and a soft place to fall, so crucial for kids, during the teen years.

Nothing like knowing that a cozy home is a waiting our teens, when they just finished a difficult day at their part time job, a new activity, or just finished up with the ACT test. She was well rested and able to focus on her test prep. Later, in college, she still took advantage of this when her schedule had breaks in it.

3. The 1:1 focus of homeschooling catches any learning gaps.

As homeschoolers, we can review, go back and switch up our curricula, or even add another year of high school, if that would help our teen.

My daughter benefited from the freedom to switch curricula or approaches when needed, gearing our homeschooling to her strengths. She was a visual learner, and we could set up her learning to focus on that, as opposed to auditory learning, and that made all the difference for her. She could work ahead on some subjects, take extra time for others.

4. Homeschooling allows for time to build special gifts, foster, and grow your teen's interests.

Following their interests motivates our teens so much, even for doing the less interesting work that would be required for their chosen field of study.

Helping our kids discover their inner-most gifts and interests, not only helps them grow, it creates strong motivation for them to learn those things that will help them in the future.

Leadership Skills

When my daughter wanted to try her hand at leading, we found activities that would foster those skills.

Homeschooling gave her the time and resources to pursue her interests in leadership. And when my daughter applied to her college honors leadership program, her high school activities helped her get accepted. More information on extracurriculars can be found in Chapter – High School Electives and Activities.

5. Interest-led learning produces motivated, self-starters.

Encouraging their interests builds self-starters! That is just what many colleges are looking for, motivated and independent learners, and those are things that makes a college student succeed.

6. Homeschooling teaches self-management skills.

Homeschoolers learn how to organize their studies, plan their days, and prioritize what needs to be done first, etc... all skills that are essential to success in college or a new vocation. Organizational skills learned at home were a key to her success during college.

7. Homeschooling teaches problem solving and researching skills.

My daughter watched me search and choose homeschool curriculum each year. During homeschool, she had often seen me search for resources, as we chose curricula, searched for a dance class, or surfed the net for help in algebra, from Khan Academy.

Through the years she learned how to problem solve and research information for herself, as she did that every day in our homeschool.

When faced with a difficult class in college, she put her problem-solving skills to work.

So her first thought, when faced with this difficult college math class was *not how she could find a way to drop it. It was, instead, a question to be answered - What resource would help me to deal with this?*

She came to me with her ideas as to how to deal with the issue... She completed the class and did well in it. Homeschooling taught her the problem-solving skills to do just that.

Those are my top 7 reasons why homeschooling prepares our teens well for college. What would you add to this list?

Chapter 17

Don't Forget the Fun!

Homeschooling high school is so much more than core studies...

Field trips, picnics, co-ops, trips to the park, exploring new interests together, getting out in nature, doing PE together, etc., are important, too. And just being there with our kids, while they are going through the all-important teen years... Isn't that why we homeschool high school anyway?

What do you enjoy doing with your teen when you need a break from it all? Especially when we were busy with all the details of college prep, SAT/ACT prep, we made time for something fun. We would stop at the park for ice cream, get the bikes out and go riding, or just head out for a walk... Whatever it was, it was important to us to make time for fun.

One of our favorite things to do was to go on mini-nature road trips. Often, we would pile in the car and go to a favorite park, nature trail, or visit a beach.

These short trips provided us with many benefits.

Having time out in nature helped us to renew ourselves, balancing out the head work that is part of homeschooling high school.

Enjoying nature means so much to my husband and I, and we are glad to be passing that onto our daughter. Meanwhile, she became quite a nature photographer, which became a long-standing hobby.

Getting out in nature became a chance to be creative and use our right brains for a change! I loved taking pictures, too.

And the hours my teen spent with the camera, became a half semester class in photography, but that was not the important thing.

She was developing a love for nature. My daughter felt relaxed talking in the car, while driving on a country road or on the way to a park. I treasure those memories, and they helped to keep our relationship strong through the busy, and sometimes challenging high school years.

Physical Education

I found that doing PE was also a great way to re-energize and also decrease stress. Any activity that helps to build up your fitness level can be included as a PE activity.

We used dance classes, free skating time, tennis camps, swimming, jogging, walking for exercise, bowling, and hiking activities for some of my daughter's PE. And doing these things together, with friends, or as a family made them all the more fun.

We kept a list of PE activities and when my teen completed 60 - 90 hours of activities, she earned one half credit in PE. Writing all the PE activities down also helped with my teen's motivation to do it! And these PE credits were accepted by all of my teen's prospective colleges.

Forms

PE Record Form - This is a form to keep track of PE Activities

May your years at home with your teen give you tons of memories to treasure, as you help them to enjoy their teen years and then take their next step in life. I have found that being a mom of a young adult is just as rich of an experience as it was to be raising them. I wish you and your family well. I leave you with a photo of my "baby" on her college graduation day.

Appendix

College Entrance Requirements Form

Overall High School Plan

Curriculum Planning Sheet

High School Credit Record Form

Sample Transcript

Instructions for Transcript Form

Official Student Transcript Form

Activities and Awards Form

Form for Homemade Courses

Community Service Log

Writing the Personal Essay

Record Keeping Form for Course Descriptions

Reference Letter Request

PE Record Form

To download and print these forms go to the **link**:

https://betsyhomeschoolconsulting.blogspot.com/2016/08/printables-for-my-new-e-book.html

College Entrance Requirements Form

College Requirements	College 1	College 2	College 3
English			
Math			
Social Studies			
Science			
Foreign Language			
Fine Arts			
Electives			

Overall High School Plan

Grade:_____	Credits		Credits
Grade:_____			
Grade:_____			
Grade:_____			

Curriculum Planning Sheet

Subject	Credits	Ideas

Homeschooling High School with College in Mind

High School Credit Record Form

Total Credits Required	Name of Course	Credits
English		
Math		
Social Studies		
Science		
Langauge		
PE, Fine Arts, Electives		

Sample Transcript

Name: Jane Smith

DOB: 8/16/96

Standarized Test Scores: Total _____

Verbal _____ Math _____ Writing _____

Date Graduated: 6/10/14

Address: 55555 Lake View Dr.

Valley City, OR 00000

Grade 9	1st	2nd	Credits
English 9	A +		1
Non-Fiction Writing	A-		1
Algebra 1	A		1
State History	B+		.5
Science 9	A	B+	1
Physical Education/Health	A		1
Photography	A	A	1
Foreign Language	A	A-	1
Grade 10	**1st**	**2nd**	**Credits**
English 10	A	A-	1
Creative Writing	A+		.5
Honors World History	A	A-	1
Biology	A	A-	1
Physical Education	A-	A-	1
Speech and Debate	A		.5
Science TA	A		.5
Geometry	B+	B+	.5
Grade 11	**1st**	**2nd**	**Credits**
American Lit and Comp	A-	A	1
US History	A-	A	1
College Planner	A	A+	.5
Art Appreciation	B+	A+	.5
Chemistry w/Lab	A-	A-	1
Algebra II	A	A-	1
Science/Community Service	A	A	.5
Physical Education	A	A-	1
Grade 12	**1st**	**2nd**	**Credits**
American Government*	B+		.5
Physics w/Lab	A-	IP	.5
British Literature	B+	IP	.5
Video Production		IP	
Introduction to Law	A+		.5
Community Service	A-		.5
Introduction to Business		IP	
Physical Education		IP	

I certify that this is a true copy of the permanent record

Total Credits:_____

GPA:_____

_____

Date   Signature   Title

A (4.0) = 90 B (3.0) = 80 C (2.0) = 70 D
(1.0)= 60 f (0/0) = 50

Homschooling High School with College in Mind

Instructions for Transcript Form

1. Fill in blanks at the top.

2. For standardized test scores, list the top scores your teen earned on either SAT/ACT like this examples: SAT: Verbal_____ Math_____Writing_____

3. List all courses including those completed at college, community college, or other outside sources. I suggest using asterisk by each outside course.

4. Figure GPA and total credits earned and note them on the transcript.

5. Sign and notarize.

NOTE: You will be sending out your teens transcripts during senior year, before their second semester courses are completed. So just note those courses as TBD (to be done) under the corresponding 1st or 2nd semester columns.

Official Transcript

Name:

DOB:

Date Graduated:

Address:

Standarized Test Scores: Total _____

Verbal _____ Math _____ Writing _____

Grade 9	1st	2nd	Credits

Grade 10	1st	2nd	Credits

Grade 11	1st	2nd	Credits

Grade 12	1st	2nd	Credits

I certify that this is a true copy of the permanent record

_____

Date   Signature   Title

Total Credits:_____

GPA:_____

A (4.0) = 90 B (3.0) = 80 C (2.0) = 70 D (1.0)= 60 f (0/0) = 50

Activities and Awards Form

Activities, Contests, Clubs, Awards, etc...	Date

Homemade Course Form

Course Name:_____

Date	Activity	Hours

Community Service Log

Date	Activity	Time

Writing the Personal Essay

Step Description	Done
Step 1 – Find the current essay prompts on the Common Application, or on your college's own application.	
Step 2 – Brainstorming	
Step 3 – Choose the Essay Prompt	
Step 4 – Make an Outline	
Step 5 – First Draft	
Step 6 – Do Revisions	
Step 7 – Final Draft	
Step 8 – Edit Spelling _____ Grammer _____ Punctuation _____ Organization _____	
Step 9 – Submit Essay	

Record Keeping Form for
Course Descriptions

Course Name	Learning activities, books, videos used, etc	Credits

Homeschooling High School with College in Mind

Reference Letter Request

Dear _____,   Date: _____

I have been participating in _____ for
_____ (Years, Months), and will soon be applying for college.

I have benefited a lot from this activity and wanted to thank you for giving
me the experiences that I have had in your program. I am applying to college
would you be willing to write a reference letter for me?

Please consider the following:
- Abilities
- Leadership Skills
- Responsibility
- Potential for success in college

Please include your title in the reference letter. Since this is a private personal
reference, I have included a stamped self-addressed envelope for each college
The colleges are listed below.

_____

_____

_____

_____

     Thank you again for all the great experiences I have received.

     Sincerely,

PE Record Form

Date	Activity	Time

About the Author

Betsy Sproger is a veteran homeschool mom and blogger who is dedicated to helping families homeschool their teens. She, along with her husband, homeschooled their dear 2e daughter from preschool through high school.

Her daughter then got into all of the colleges on her list with scholarship offers, including a tier one university. Four years later, she graduated Cum Laude. Betsy shares that just to encourage you and other families who have college bound teens.

She blogs at BJ's Homeschool, sharing resources and encouragement for homeschooling high school and college, with some focus also on special needs and learning differences.

Betsy has served on the author board for *The Curriculum Choice* for many years and is a member of the iHomeschool Network. She is also on the writing team of the *Gifted Homeschooler Forum* and the *Hoagies Gifted Education Page.*

Betsy is a former OT and preschool teacher who loves gardening, hiking, nature photography and enjoying her beloved Pacific NW, with her husband and daughter. She would love for their cat to join them on their hikes, but as of yet that has not happened.

Homeschooling High School with College in Mind was awarded the *Lit Pick's* 5 Star award in January 2019.

CPSIA information can be obtained
at www.ICGtesting.com
Printed in the USA
BVHW011616130720
583593BV00006B/430